"Here's a book that every preacher should read at least once a year. This book is a powerful antidote to the unbalanced, self-centered preaching of today."

Erwin W. Lutzer, Pastor Emeritus, The Moody Church, Chicago

"This book calls us back to a biblical standard for preaching, a standard exemplified by many of the pulpit giants of the past, especially Jonathan Edwards and Charles Spurgeon."

Warren W. Wiersbe, Former General Director, Back to the Bible

"The Bible is not a book of practical suggestions on how to live a better adjusted life. The Bible is a revelation of God. *The Supremacy of God in Preaching* reminds preachers of what we easily forget to our peril and the peril of the people in our care."

Haddon Robinson, Former Professor of Preaching, Gordon-Conwell Theological Seminary

"Occasionally, among the myriad of books for ministers, a work appears so seminal to the preacher's calling that it can safely be said: 'This is a must-read.' *The Supremacy of God in Preaching* is such a book."

Sinclair Ferguson, Chancellor's Professor of Systematic Theology, Reformed Theological Seminary; Teaching Fellow, Ligonier Ministries

"*The Supremacy of God in Preaching* is one of the few truly indispensable books on gospel ministry."

Philip Graham Ryken, President, Wheaton College

"John Piper passionately and prophetically calls all preachers to make God supreme over any method and in every message. The plan is too simple for a fallen world to notice and too powerful for a faithful preacher to ignore."

Bryan Chapell, Pastor Emeritus, Grace Presbyterian Church, Peoria, Illinois

The Supremacy of God in Preaching

Other Books by John Piper

Battling Unbelief

Bloodlines

Brothers, We Are Not Professionals

Coronavirus and Christ

The Dangerous Duty of Delight

Desiring God

Does God Desire All to Be Saved?

Don't Waste Your Life

Expository Exultation

Fifty Reasons Why Jesus Came to Die

Finally Alive

Five Points

Future Grace

God Is the Gospel

God's Passion for His Glory

A Godward Heart

A Godward Life

A Hunger for God

Lessons from a Hospital Bed

Let the Nations Be Glad!

A Peculiar Glory

The Pleasures of God

Reading the Bible Supernaturally

Seeing and Savoring Jesus Christ

Spectacular Sins

A Sweet and Bitter Providence

Taste and See

Think

This Momentary Marriage

What Jesus Demands from the World

When I Don't Desire God

Why I Love the Apostle Paul

The Supremacy of God in Preaching

John Piper

Revised and Expanded Edition

CROSSWAY®

WHEATON, ILLINOIS

Cover Design: Jordan Singer
Cover Image: *Sunrise on the Matterhorn* by Albert Bierstadt / The Metropolitan Museum of Art
First printing, 2021
Printed in the United States of America

Hardcover ISBN: 978-1-4335-7284-5

Library of Congress Cataloging-in-Publication Data
Names: Piper, John, 1946– author.
Title: The supremacy of God in preaching / John Piper.
Description: Revised edition. | Wheaton, Illinois: Crossway, 2021. | Includes bibliographical references and index.
Identifiers: LCCN 2020031628 | ISBN 9781433572845 (hardback)
Subjects: LCSH: Preaching. | Clergy—Religious life. | Edwards, Jonathan, 1703–1758.
Classification: LCC BV4211.3 .P57 2021 | DDC 251—dc23
LC record available at https://lccn.loc.gov/2020031628

Crossway is a publishing ministry of Good News Publishers.

SH			29	28	27	26	25	24	23	22	21
14	13	12	11	10	9	8	7	6	5	4	3	2	1

To the people of

Bethlehem Baptist Church

*who share the vision
of spreading a passion
for the supremacy of God in all things
for the joy of all peoples
through Jesus Christ*

Contents

Preface to the Revised and Expanded Edition

GOD IS STILL THE MOST IMPORTANT, most valuable, most satisfying, most all-encompassing, and, therefore, most relevant reality in the world. So a little book that focuses on the relationship between his supremacy and preaching is still relevant. Twenty-five years after I first wrote it, this is still what I want to say. It was my focus as I began my pastoral ministry in 1980, and it was my focus to the end, as I concluded that ministry on Easter Sunday, March 31, 2013.

So in this edition, I have added four new chapters in a section called "After Thirty-Three Years: God Still Supreme in Preaching and Ministry." One chapter extends my exultation over Jonathan Edwards into my seventh decade. He was seminal for me in my twenties. He is still teaching me and inspiring me in my sixties.

The second new chapter celebrates the freedom, authority, and power that comes with preaching that is tethered to the Word of God. I contrast the Bible-oriented preacher with the entertainment-oriented preacher, and plead for connections between bold sermons and biblical texts that people can actually see and bank on. After thirty-three years, the Bible is more real, more powerful, more al-luring, more joy-giving, and more inexhaustible to me than it has ever been. To preach as though anything else is more interesting, more insightful, or more satisfying is a symptom of soul-sickness. The third new chapter is a brief reflection on the issue of contextualization in preaching. The point is that we should give as much energy to creating new categories in the minds of our listeners as we should to trying to find existent categories to contain the mind-boggling realities of Scripture. Both efforts are crucial. But category creation is the hardest—namely, impossible. It is the work of the Holy Spirit. But he uses our thinking and preaching to bring it about.

The final new chapter is a litany of wonders at the privilege of being a pastor. It's called "Thirty Reasons Why It Is a Great Thing to Be a Pastor." This is my tribute to the mercy of God in granting me the unspeakable privilege of being carried in pastoral ministry for so long. I look back with stunned amazement that he kept me and gave me a people of such patience. Their love covered a multitude of sins.

I pray that this revised and expanded edition will encourage veteran pastors and will help launch young pastors on a lifetime of God-centered, Christ-exalting, Bible-saturated devotion to heralding the supremacy of God in all things for the joy of all peoples through Jesus Christ.

John Piper
February 2014

Preface to the Revised Edition

MORE THAN EVER I BELIEVE IN preaching as a part of worship in the gathered church. Preaching is worship, and it belongs in the regular worship life of the church no matter the size of the church. In the small church it does not become conversation or "sharing." In the megachurch it does not become hype and jingles. Preaching is worshiping over the Word of God—the text of Scripture—with explanation and exultation.

Preaching belongs in the corporate worship of the church not only because the New Testament commands "preach the word" (*kēruxon ton logon*) in the context of body life (2 Tim. 3:16–4:2), but even more fundamentally because the twofold essence of worship demands it. This twofold essence of worship comes from God's way of revealing himself to us. Jonathan Edwards puts it like this:

> God glorifies Himself toward the creatures also in two ways:
> 1. By appearing to their understanding. 2. In communicating Himself to their hearts, and in their rejoicing and delighting in and enjoying the manifestations which He makes of Himself.
> . . . *God is glorified not only by His glory's being seen, but by its*

being rejoiced in. When those that see it delight in it, God is more glorified than if they only see it. His glory is then received by the whole soul, both by the understanding and by the heart.[1]

There are always two parts to true worship. There is *seeing* God and there is *savoring* God. You can't separate these. You must see him to savor him. And if you don't savor him when you see him, you insult him. In true worship, there is always *understanding* with the mind and there is always *feeling* in the heart. Understanding must always be the foundation of feeling, or all we have is baseless emotionalism. But understanding of God that doesn't give rise to feeling for God becomes mere intellectualism and deadness. This is why the Bible continually calls us to think and consider and meditate, on the one hand, and to rejoice and fear and mourn and delight and hope and be glad, on the other hand. Both are essential for worship.

The reason the Word of God takes the form of preaching in worship is that true preaching is the kind of speech that consistently unites these two aspects of worship, both in the way it is done and in the aims that it has. When Paul says to Timothy in 2 Timothy 4:2, "Preach the word," the term he uses for "preach" is a word for "herald" or "announce" or "proclaim" (*kēruxon*). It is not a word for "teach" or "explain." It is what a town crier did: "Hear ye, hear ye, hear ye! The King has a proclamation of good news for all those who swear allegiance to his throne. Be it known to you that he will give eternal life to all who trust and love his Son." I call this heralding *exultation.* Preaching is a public exultation over the truth that it brings. It is not disinterested or cool or neutral. It is not mere explanation. It is manifestly and contagiously passionate about what it says.

Nevertheless this heralding contains teaching. You can see that as you look back to 2 Timothy 3:16—the Scripture (which gives rise to preaching) is profitable for *teaching*. And you can see it as you look ahead to the rest of 2 Timothy 4:2, "Preach the word . . . reprove, rebuke, and exhort, with complete patience and teaching." So preaching is expository. It deals with the Word of God. True preaching is not the opinions of a mere man. It is the faithful exposition of God's Word. So in a phrase, preaching is *expository exultation*.

In conclusion, then, the reason that preaching is so essential to the corporate worship of the church is that it is uniquely suited to feed both *understanding* and *feeling*. It is uniquely suited to waken *seeing* God and *savoring* God. God has ordained that the Word of God come in a form that teaches the mind and reaches the heart.

May God use this revised edition of *The Supremacy of God in Preaching* to advance a movement of God-centered worship and life. May the preaching of our churches more and more show the truth of Christ and savor the glory of Christ. May the pulpits of the land ring with exposition of the Word of God and exultation in the God of the Word.

John Piper
2003

Preface to the First Edition

PEOPLE ARE STARVING FOR the greatness of God. But most of them would not give this diagnosis of their troubled lives. The majesty of God is an unknown cure. There are far more popular prescriptions on the market, but the benefit of any other remedy is brief and shallow. Preaching that does not have the aroma of God's greatness may entertain for a season, but it will not touch the hidden cry of the soul: "Show me thy glory!" Years ago during the January prayer week at our church, I decided to preach on the holiness of God from Isaiah 6. I resolved on the first Sunday of the year to unfold the vision of God's holiness found in the first four verses of that chapter:

> In the year that King Uzziah died I saw the Lord sitting upon a throne, high and lifted up; and the train of his robe filled the temple. Above him stood the seraphim. Each had six wings: with two he covered his face, and with two he covered his feet, and with two he flew. And one called to another and said:
>
> > "Holy, holy, holy is the Lord of hosts;
> > the whole earth is full of his glory!"

And the foundations of the thresholds shook at the voice of him who called, and the house was filled with smoke.

So I preached on the holiness of God and did my best to display the majesty and glory of such a great and holy God. I gave not one word of application to the lives of our people. Application is essential in the normal course of preaching, but I felt led that day to make a test: Would the passionate portrayal of the greatness of God in and of itself meet the needs of people?

I didn't realize that not long before this Sunday one of the young families of our church discovered that their child was being sexually abused by a close relative. It was incredibly traumatic. They were there that Sunday morning and sat under that message. I wonder how many advisers to us pastors today would have said, "Pastor Piper, can't you see your people are hurting? Can't you come down out of the heavens and get practical? Don't you realize what kind of people sit in front of you on Sunday?" Some weeks later I learned the story. The husband took me aside one Sunday after a service. "John, these have been the hardest months of our lives. Do you know what has gotten me through? The vision of the greatness of God's holiness that you gave me the first week of January. It has been the rock we could stand on."

The greatness and the glory of God are relevant. It does not matter if surveys turn up a list of perceived needs that does not include the supreme greatness of the sovereign God of grace. That is the deepest need. Our people are starving for God.

Another illustration of this is the way missions mobilization has happened at our church and the way it has happened again and again in history. Younger people today don't get fired up about denominations and agencies. They get fired up about the greatness of a global God and about the unstoppable purpose of a sovereign King. The first great missionary said, "We have received grace and apostleship to bring about the obedience of faith *for the sake of his name* among all the nations" (Rom. 1:5). Missions is for the sake of the name of God. It flows from a love for God's glory and for the honor of his reputation. It is an answer to the prayer, "Hallowed be thy name!"

So I am persuaded that the vision of a great God is the linchpin in the life of the church, both in pastoral care and missionary outreach. Our people need to hear God-entranced preaching. They need someone, at least once a week, to lift up his voice and magnify the supremacy of God. They need to see the whole panorama of his excellencies. Robert Murray M'Cheyne said, "What my people need most is my personal holiness."[1] That's right. But human holiness is nothing other than a God-besotted life—the living out of a God-entranced worldview.

God himself is the necessary subject matter of our preaching, in his majesty and truth and holiness and righteousness and wisdom and faithfulness and sovereignty and grace. And by that I don't mean we shouldn't preach about nitty-gritty practical things like parenthood and divorce and AIDS and gluttony and television and sex. What I mean is that every one of those things should be swept right up into the holy presence of God and laid bare to the roots of its Godwardness or godlessness.

It is not the job of the Christian preacher to give people moral or psychological pep talks about how to get along in the world. When that is needed, someone else can do it. But most of our people have no one, no one in the world, to tell them, week in and week out, about the supreme beauty and majesty of God. And so many of them are tragically starved for the God-entranced vision of that great old preacher Jonathan Edwards.

Church historian Mark Noll describes the tragedy like this:

> Since Edwards, American evangelicals have not thought about life from the ground up as Christians because their entire culture has ceased to do so. Edwards's *piety* continued on in the revivalist tradition, his *theology* continued on in academic Calvinism, but there were no successors to his God-entranced world-view or his profoundly theological philosophy. The disappearance of Edwards's perspective in American Christian history has been a tragedy.[2]

Charles Colson echoes this conviction:

> The western church—much of it drifting, enculturated, and infected with cheap grace—desperately needs to hear Edwards' challenge. . . . It is my belief that the prayers and work of those who love and obey Christ in our world may yet prevail as they keep the message of such a man as Jonathan Edwards.[3]

The recovery of Edwards's "God-entranced world-view" in the messengers of God would be a cause of great rejoicing in the land and profound thanksgiving to the God who makes all things new.

The chapters in Part 1 were first delivered as the Harold John Ockenga Lectures on Preaching at Gordon-Conwell Theological Seminary in February 1988. The chapters in Part 2 were first given as the Billy Graham Center Lectures on Preaching at Wheaton College in October 1984. This privilege and effort was far greater gain to me than anyone else. I give public thanks to the administrative leaders at these schools who trusted me in this way and stretched my own grasp of the high calling of the Christian preacher.

I continually thank God that he has never left me on a Sunday morning without a word to speak and a zeal to speak it for his glory. Oh, I have my moods. My family of four sons [and a daughter since the first edition] and a steady wife is not without its pain and tears. Letters of criticism can stab to the quick. Discouragement can go so deep as to leave this preacher numb. But it is a gift of measureless, sovereign grace that, beyond all desert and all adequacy, God has opened his Word to me and given me a heart to savor it and send it forth week after week. I have never ceased to love to preach.

In the mercy of God there is a human reason for this. Charles Spurgeon knew it, and most happy preachers know it. Once, while visiting the continent, Spurgeon was asked about the secret of his ministry. After a moment's pause Mr. Spurgeon said, "My people pray for me."[4] This is why I have not ceased to love to preach. This is why I have been revived again and again for the work of the ministry. With all its weaknesses and imperfections owing to me, this is how *The Supremacy of God in Preaching* came to be written. My people pray for me. To them I dedicate this book with affection and gratitude.

My prayer is that the book may turn the hearts of God's heralds to the fulfillment of this great apostolic admonition:

Whoever speaks, [let it be] as one who speaks oracles of God . . . by the strength that God supplies—in order that in everything God may be glorified through Jesus Christ. To him belong glory and dominion forever and ever. Amen. (1 Pet. 4:11)

John Piper
1990

PART 1

_____

WHY GOD SHOULD BE SUPREME IN PREACHING

1

The Goal of Preaching

The Glory of God

IN SEPTEMBER 1966 I was a junior at Wheaton College. I was a pre-med student majoring in literature. I had just finished a chemistry course in summer school, was head over heels in love with Noël (now my wife of more than thirty-five years), and was more sick than I have ever been before or after, with mononucleosis. The doctor confined me to the health center for three weeks—three of the most decisive weeks of my life, for which I do not cease to thank God.

Back in those days the fall semester began with a "Spiritual Emphasis Week." The speaker in 1966 was Harold John Ockenga. It was the first and last time I ever heard him preach. WETN, the college radio station, carried the sermons, and I listened as I lay on my bed two hundred yards from his pulpit. Under the preaching of the Word by Pastor Ockenga, the direction of my life was permanently changed. I can remember my heart almost bursting with longing as I listened—longing to know and handle the Word of God like that. Through those messages God called me to the ministry of the Word irresistibly, and I believe, irrevocably. It has been my conviction ever since that the subjective evidence of God's call to the ministry of the Word (to use the words of Charles Spurgeon) "is an intense, all-absorbing desire for the work."[1]

When I got out of the health center, I dropped organic chemistry, took up philosophy as a minor, and set my face to get the best biblical and theological education I could. Almost forty years later I can testify that the Lord has never let me doubt that call. It rings as clear in my heart today as it ever has. And I simply stand in awe at the gracious providence of God—to save me and call me as a servant of the Word, and then two decades later to let me speak under the banner of "The Harold John Ockenga Lectures on Preaching" at Gordon-Conwell Theological Seminary.

That was a precious privilege for me. And I prayed that it would be an acceptable tribute to Dr. Ockenga, who never knew me—and therefore a testimony to the fact that the true usefulness of our preaching will not be known to us until all the fruit on all the branches on all the trees that have sprung up from all the seeds we've ever sown has fully ripened in the sunshine of eternity.

> For as the rain and the snow come down from heaven
> and do not return there but water the earth,
> making it bring forth and sprout,
> giving seed to the sower and bread to the eater,
> so shall my word be that goes out from my mouth;
> it shall not return to me empty,
> but it shall accomplish that which I purpose,
> and shall succeed in the thing for which I sent it.
> (Isa. 55:10–11)

Dr. Ockenga never knew what his preaching did in my life. And you can mark it down: God will hide from you much of your fruit. You will see enough to be assured of his blessing, but not so much as to think you could live without it. For God aims to exalt himself, not the preacher, in this affair of preaching. And that brings us to the theme: the supremacy of God in preaching. Its outline is intentionally Trinitarian:

The Goal of Preaching: The Glory of God
The Ground of Preaching: The Cross of Christ
The Gift of Preaching: The Power of the Holy Spirit

God the Father, God the Son, and God the Holy Spirit are the beginning, middle, and end in the ministry of preaching. Written over all ministerial labor, especially preaching, stand the words of the apostle: "From him and through him and to him are all things. To him be glory forever" (Rom. 11:36).

The Scottish preacher James Stewart put it like this: the aims of all genuine preaching are "to quicken the conscience by the holiness of God, to feed the mind with the truth of God, to purge the imagination by the beauty of God, to open the heart to the love of God, to devote the will to the purpose of God."[2] In other words, God is the goal of preaching, God is the ground of preaching, and all the means in between are given by the Spirit of God.

My burden in these pages is to plead for the supremacy of God in preaching—that the *dominant note* of preaching be the freedom of God's sovereign grace, that the *unifying theme* be the zeal that God has for his own glory, that the *grand object* of preaching be the infinite and inexhaustible being of God, and that the *pervasive atmosphere* of preaching be the holiness of God. Then when preaching takes up the ordinary things of life (family, job, leisure, friendships) or the crises of our day (AIDS, divorce, addictions, depression, abuses, poverty, hunger, and, worst of all, unreached peoples of the world), these matters are not only taken up—they are taken all the way up into God.

John Henry Jowett, who preached for thirty-four years in England and America until 1923, saw this as the great power of Robert Dale and Horace Bushnell and John Newman and Charles Spurgeon. He says:

> They were always willing to stop at the village window, but they always linked the streets with the heights, and sent your souls a-roaming over the eternal hills of God. . . . It is this note of vastitude, this ever-present sense and suggestion of the Infinite, which I think we need to recover in our preaching.[3]

Here we are a century later and the need for that recovery is ten times as great.

Nor am I talking here about a kind of artsy elitist preoccupation with philosophical or intellectual imponderables. There are aesthetic types who gravitate to high church services because they can't stand the slapstick of many evangelical worship services. But that is not what I am calling for. Charles Spurgeon was anything but an intellectual elitist. There has scarcely been a pastor with more popular appeal. But his messages were full of God, and the atmosphere was charged with the presence of awesome realities. "We shall never have great preachers," he said, "till we have great divines."[4]

That wasn't because he cared more about great ideas than lost souls. He cared about the one because he loved the other. It was the same with Isaac Watts, who lived a hundred years earlier. Samuel

Johnson said of Watts, "Whatever he took in hand, was, by his incessant solicitude for souls, converted to theology."[5] Which I take to mean, in Watts's case, that everything was brought into relation to God—because he cared about people.

Today Johnson would, I believe, say of much contemporary preaching, "Whatever the preacher takes in his hand, is, by his incessant solicitude for relevance, converted to psychology." And neither the great aims of preaching nor the worthy place of psychology is honored in this loss of theological nerve. My guess is that one great reason why people sometimes doubt the abiding value of God-centered preaching is because they have never heard any. J. I. Packer tells about how he heard the preaching of Martyn Lloyd-Jones every Sunday evening at Westminster Chapel during 1948 and '49. He said that he had never heard such preaching. It came to him with the force and surprise of electric shock. Lloyd-Jones, he said, brought him "more of a sense of God than any other man."[6]

Is this what people take away from worship nowadays—a sense of God? A note of sovereign grace, a theme of panoramic glory, the grand object of God's infinite Being? Do they enter for one hour in the week—not an excessive expectation—into an atmosphere of the holiness of God, which leaves its aroma upon their lives all week long?

Cotton Mather, who ministered in New England three hundred years ago, said, "The great design and intention of the office of a Christian preacher [is] to restore the throne and dominion of God in the souls of men."[7] And that was not a rhetorical flourish. It was a measured and accurate exegetical conclusion from one of the great biblical texts on preaching, which leads to the biblical foundation for God's supremacy in preaching. The text behind Mather's statement is Romans 10:14–15:

How then will they call on him in whom they have not believed? And how are they to believe in him of whom they have never heard? And how are they to hear without someone preaching? And how are they to preach unless they are sent? As it is written, "How beautiful are the feet of those who preach the good news!"

From this text *preaching* could be defined as "the heralding of good news from a messenger sent by God" ("heralding"—from the word *kērussontos* in v. 14; "of good news"—from *euangelizomenōn agatha* in v. 15; "sent by a sent messenger"—from *apostalōsin* in v. 15).

But the key question now is, What does the preacher herald? What is the good news referred to here? Since verse 16 is a quotation of Isaiah 52:7, we do well to go back and let Isaiah define it for us. Listen for what Cotton Mather heard in this verse concerning the great design of Christian preaching.

How beautiful upon the mountains
　　are the feet of him who brings good news,
who publishes peace, who brings good news of happiness,
　　who publishes salvation,
　　who says to Zion, "Your God reigns."

The good tidings of the preacher, the peace and salvation that he publishes, are boiled down into one sentence: "Your God reigns!" Cotton Mather applies this, with full justification, to the preacher: "The great design . . . of a Christian preacher [is] to restore the throne and dominion of God in the souls of men."

The keynote in the mouth of every prophet-preacher, whether in Isaiah's day or Jesus's day or our day, is "Your God reigns!" God is the king of the universe. He has absolute Creator rights over this world and everyone in it. But there is rebellion and mutiny on all sides, and his authority is scorned by millions. So the Lord sends preachers into the world to cry out that God reigns, that he will not suffer his glory to be scorned indefinitely, that he will vindicate his name in great and terrible wrath, but that for now a full and free amnesty is offered to all the rebel subjects who will turn from their rebellion, call on him for mercy, bow before his throne, and swear allegiance and fealty to him forever. The amnesty is signed in the blood of his Son.

So Mather is absolutely right: The grand design of the Christian preacher is to restore the throne and dominion of God in the souls of men. But why? Can we go deeper? What is driving the heart of God in demanding that we submit to his authority and in offering the mercy of amnesty?

Isaiah gives the answer in an earlier text, Isaiah 48:9–11. Speaking of his mercy to Israel, God says:

> For my name's sake I defer my anger,
>> for the sake of my praise I restrain it for you,
>> that I may not cut you off.
> Behold, I have refined you, but not as silver;
>> I have tried you in the furnace of affliction.
> For my own sake, for my own sake, I do it,
>> for how should my name be profaned?
>> My glory I will not give to another.

Behind and beneath the sovereign exercises of God's mercy as king is an unwavering passion for the honor of his name and the display of his glory.

So we can go deeper than Mather's point. Behind God's commitment to reign as king is the deeper foundational commitment that his glory will one day fill the earth (Num. 14:21; Ps. 57:5; 72:19; Isa. 11:9; Hab. 2:14). And this discovery has a tremendous implication for preaching. God's deepest purpose for the world is to fill the earth with reverberations of his glory in the lives of a new humanity ransomed from every people and tribe and tongue and nation (Rev. 5:9).[8] But the glory of God does not reflect brightly in the hearts of men and women when they cower unwillingly in submission to his authority, or when they obey in servile fear, or when there is no gladness in response to the glory of their king.

The implication for preaching is plain: When God sends his emissaries to declare, "Your God reigns!" his aim is not to constrain man's submission by an act of raw authority; his aim is to ravish our affections with irresistible displays of glory. The only submission that fully reflects the worth and glory of the king is glad submission. Begrudging submission berates the king. No gladness in the subject, no glory to the king.

This is what Jesus said in effect in Matthew 13:44: "The kingdom [the rule, the dominion] of heaven is like a treasure hidden in a field, which a man found and covered up. Then in his joy [his glad submission to that kingship and his delight in its glory, its value] he went and sold all that he had to buy that field." When the kingdom is a treasure, submission is a pleasure. Or to turn it around, when submission is a pleasure, the kingdom is glorified as a treasure. Therefore, if the goal of preaching is to glorify God, it must aim at glad submission to his kingdom, not raw submission.

Paul said in 2 Corinthians 4:5, "What we proclaim is not ourselves, but Jesus Christ as Lord." But then in verse 6 he goes beneath that proclamation of the Lordship of Christ—beneath the rule and authority of King Jesus—and tells the essence of his preaching: It is "the light of the knowledge of the glory of God in the face of Jesus Christ." The only submission to the Lordship of Christ that fully magnifies his worth and reflects his beauty is the humble gladness of the human soul in the glory of God in the face of his Son.

The wonder of the gospel, and the most freeing discovery this sinner has ever made, is that God's deepest commitment to be glorified and my deepest longing to be satisfied are not in conflict, but in fact find simultaneous consummation in his display of and my delight in the glory of God.[9] Therefore, the goal of preaching is the glory of God reflected in the glad submission of the human heart. And the supremacy of God in preaching is secured by this fact: The one who satisfies gets the glory; the one who gives the pleasure is the treasure.

2

The Ground of Preaching

The Cross of Christ

PREACHING IS THE HERALDING of the good news by a messenger sent by God. The good news . . .

> that God reigns;
>
> that he reigns to reveal his glory;
>
> that his glory is revealed most fully in the glad submission of his creation;
>
> that, therefore, there is no final conflict between God's zeal to be glorified and our longing to be satisfied;
>
> and that someday the earth will be filled with the glory of the Lord, echoing and reverberating in the white-hot worship of the ransomed church gathered in from every people and tongue and tribe and nation.

The goal of preaching is the glory of God in Christ reflected in the glad submission of his creation.

But there are two massive obstacles to the attainment of this goal: the righteousness of God and the pride of man. The righteousness of God is his unwavering zeal for the exaltation of his own glory.[1] And the pride of man is his unwavering zeal for the exaltation of man's glory.

What in God is righteousness, in man is sin. This is the very point of Genesis 3—that sin came into the world through a temptation, and that the essence of that temptation was, "You will be like God." The effort to imitate God at this point is the essence of our corruption.

Our parents fell for it, and in them we have all fallen for it. It's now part of our nature. We take the mirror of God's image, which was intended to reflect his glory in the world, and turn our backs to the light, and fall in love with the contours of our own dark shadow, trying desperately to convince ourselves (with technological advances or management skills or athletic prowess or academic achievements or sexual exploits or counterculture hair styles) that the dark shadow of the image on the ground in front of us is really glorious and satisfying. And in our proud love affair with ourselves, we pour contempt (whether we know it or not!) on the worth of God's glory.

And as our pride pours contempt upon God's glory, his righteousness obliges him to pour wrath upon our pride.

The haughty looks of man shall be brought low,
and the lofty pride of men shall be humbled;
and the Lord alone will be exalted in that day.
For how should my name be profaned?
My glory I will not give to another.
The eyes of the haughty are brought low . . .

and the Holy God shows himself holy in righteousness.
Destruction is decreed, overflowing with righteousness.
  (Isa. 2:11; 48:11; 5:15–16; 10:22)

The goal of preaching is the glory of God in the glad submission of his creation. And so there is an obstacle to this preaching in God, and there is an obstacle in man. The pride of man will not delight in God's glory. The righteousness of God will not suffer his glory to be scorned.

So where is there any hope that preaching might attain its goal—that God be glorified in those who are satisfied in him? Can the righteousness of God ever relent in its opposition to sinners? Can the pride of man ever be broken of its own vanity and be satisfied in God's glory? Is there a basis for such hope? Is there a ground for valid and hopeful preaching?

There is. In the cross of Christ, God has undertaken to overcome both obstacles to preaching. It overcomes the objective, external obstacle of God's righteous opposition to human pride. And it overcomes the subjective, internal obstacle of our proud opposition to God's glory. In so doing the cross becomes the ground of the objective validity of preaching and the ground of the subjective humility of preaching.

Let's take these one at a time and look at the biblical evidence.

1. The Cross as the Ground of the Validity of Preaching

The most fundamental problem of preaching is how a preacher can proclaim hope to sinners in view of God's unimpeachable righteousness. Of course, man by himself does not view this as the most serious problem. He never has.

I recall listening to a tape by R. C. Sproul a few years ago that made this point powerfully. It was called "The Misplaced Locus of Amazement." It was a sermon on Luke 13:1–5. Some people came to Jesus and told him about the Galileans whose blood Pilate had mingled with their sacrifices. Jesus responded in shockingly unsentimental words: "Do you think that these Galileans were worse sinners than all the other Galileans, because they suffered in this way? No, I tell you; but unless you repent, you will all likewise perish." In other words, Jesus says, "Are you amazed that a few Galileans were killed by Pilate? What you ought to be amazed at is that all of you haven't been killed, and that you will be someday if you don't repent."

Sproul pointed out that here you have the age-old difference between the way natural man sees the problem of his relation to God and the way the Bible sees the problem of man's relation to God. Man-centered humans are amazed that God should withhold life and joy from his creatures. But the God-centered Bible is amazed that God should withhold judgment from sinners. One of the implications this has for preaching is that preachers who take their cue from the Bible and not from the world will always be wrestling with spiritual realities that many of their hearers do not even know exist or think essential. But the main point here is this: that the fundamental problem with preaching, whether a man-centered age like ours feels it or not, is how a preacher can proclaim hope to sinners in view of God's unimpeachable righteousness.

And the glorious solution to that problem is the cross of Christ. It is explained most clearly for us in Romans 3:23–26.

All have sinned and fall short of the glory of God [they exchanged the glory of God for the glory of the creature (1:23)], and are justified by his grace as a gift, through the redemption that is in Christ Jesus, whom God put forward as a propitiation by his blood [there's the cross!], to be received by faith. This was to show God's righteousness, because in his divine forbearance he had passed over former sins. It was to show his righteousness at the present time, so that he might be just and the justifier of the one who has faith in Jesus.

What this amazing passage says is that the fundamental problem of preaching has been overcome by the cross. Without the cross, the righteousness of God would demonstrate itself only in the condemnation of sinners, and the goal of preaching would abort—God would not be glorified in the gladness of his sinful creatures. His righteousness would simply be vindicated in their destruction.

What the text teaches is that—even though all scorn the glory of God (according to Rom. 3:23), and even though God's righteousness is his unwavering commitment to uphold that glory (implied in 3:25)—nevertheless, God designed a way to vindicate the worth of his glory and at the same time give hope to sinners who have scorned that glory—and what he designed was the death of his Son. It took the infinitely costly death of the Son of God to repair the dishonor that my pride has brought upon the glory of God.

It horribly skews the meaning of the cross when contemporary prophets of self-esteem say that the cross is a witness to my infinite worth, since God was willing to pay such a high price to get me. The biblical perspective is that the cross is a witness to the infinite worth of God's glory and a witness to the immensity of the sin of my pride. What should shock us is that we have brought such contempt upon the worth of God that the very death of his Son is required to vindicate that worth. The cross witnesses to the infinite worth of God and the infinite outrage of sin.

Now I hope you can see in all this that what God achieved in the cross of Christ is the warrant or ground of preaching. Preaching would not be valid without the cross. The goal of preaching would contain an irresolvable contradiction—the glory of a righteous God magnified in the gladness of a sinful people. But the cross has brought together the two sides of the goal of preaching that looked hopelessly at odds with each other: (1) the vindication and exaltation of God's glory and (2) the hope and joy and gladness of sinful man.

In chapter 1 we saw that preaching is the heralding of the good news that God's zeal to be glorified and our longing to be satisfied are not in final conflict. And what we have seen so far in this chapter is that the ground of this proclamation is the cross of Christ. This is the gospel beneath all the other things preaching has to say. Without the cross, preaching that aims to glorify a righteous God in the gladness of sinful man has no validity.

So we turn now from the cross as the ground of the validity of preaching to . . .

2. The Cross as the Ground of the Humility of Preaching

The cross is also the ground of the humility of preaching because the cross is the power of God to crucify the pride of both preacher and congregation. In the New Testament the cross is not only a past place of objective substitution; it is also a present place of subjective execution—the execution of my self-reliance and my love affair with the praise of man. "Far be it from me to boast except in the cross of our Lord Jesus Christ, by which the world has been crucified to me, and I to the world" (Gal. 6:14).

The point where Paul made the most of this crucifying power of the cross was in relation to his own preaching. I doubt that there is a more important passage on preaching in all the Bible than the first and second chapters of 1 Corinthians, where Paul shows that the great obstacle to the aims of preaching in Corinth was pride. The people were enamored with oratorical skill and intellectual prowess and philosophical airs. They lined up behind their favorite teachers and boasted in men: "I follow Paul!" "I follow Apollos!" "I follow Cephas!"

Paul's aim in these chapters is stated negatively in 1:29, "That no human being might boast in the presence of God," and positively in 1:31, "Let the one who boasts, boast in the Lord." In other words, Paul will not deny us the great satisfaction that comes from exulting in glory and reveling in greatness. We were made for that very pleasure. But neither will he deny to God the glory and the greatness that echo back to him when people boast in the Lord and not man. Glut your desire to boast by boasting in the Lord.

Paul's aims are the aims of Christian preaching—the glory of God in the glad-hearted, Godward boast of the Corinthian Christians. But pride stands in the way. And to remove it Paul talks about the effect of the cross on his own preaching. His main point is that the "word of the cross" (1:18) is the power of God to break the pride of man—both preacher and listener—and bring us to a glad reliance on the mercy of God and not on ourselves.

Let me give you just a few examples of this from the text: "For Christ did not send me to baptize but to preach the gospel, and not with words of eloquent wisdom, lest the cross of Christ be emptied of its power" (1:17). Why would the cross have been emptied if Paul had come with oratorical flourishes and displays of philosophical wisdom? It would have been emptied because he would have been cultivating the very boasting in man that the cross was meant to crucify. This is what I mean when I say that the cross is the ground of the humility of preaching.

Consider the same point in 2:1: "I, when I came to you, brothers, did not come proclaiming to you the testimony of God with lofty speech or wisdom." In other words, he avoided the ostentation of oratory and intellect. Why? What was the ground of this demeanor in preaching? Verse 2 tells us very plainly: "For I decided to know nothing among you except Jesus Christ and him crucified."

I think what he means by this verse is that he set his mind to be so saturated with the crucifying power of the cross that in everything he said and did, in all his preaching, there would be the aroma of death—death to self-reliance, death to pride, death to boasting in man—so that the life that people would see would be the life of Christ, and the power that people would see would be the power of God.

Why? Why did he want people to see this and not himself? Verse 5 answers: "So that your faith might not rest in the wisdom of men but in the power of God." In other words, that God (not the preacher!) might be honored in the trust of his people. That's the goal of preaching!

So I conclude that the cross of Christ not only provides a foundation for the validity of preaching—enabling us to herald the good news that a righteous God can and will be glorified in the glad submission of sinners—but also provides a foundation for the humility of preaching.

The cross is both a past event of substitution and a present experience of execution. It holds up the glory of God in preaching, and it holds down the pride of man in the preacher. It is the foundation of our doctrine and the foundation of our demeanor.

Paul goes so far as to say that unless the preacher is crucified, the preaching is nullified (1 Cor. 1:17). What we are in preaching is utterly crucial to what we say. This is why I turn in chapter 3 to the enabling power of the Holy Spirit and in chapter 4 to the gravity and gladness of preaching.

3

The Gift of Preaching

The Power of the Holy Spirit

THE SUPREMACY OF GOD in preaching demands that displaying and magnifying God's glory be our constant goal in preaching (chapter 1), that the all-sufficiency of the cross of God's Son be the conscious validation of our preaching and humiliation of our pride (chapter 2), and that the sovereign work of the Spirit of God be the power in which all this is achieved (this chapter).

How utterly dependent we are on the Holy Spirit in the work of preaching! All genuine preaching is rooted in a feeling of desperation. You wake up on Sunday morning and you can smell the smoke of hell on one side and feel the crisp breezes of heaven on the other. You go to your study and look down at your pitiful manuscript, and you kneel down and cry, "O God, this is so weak! Who do I think I am? What audacity to think that in three hours my words will be the odor of death to death and the fragrance of life to life (2 Cor. 2:16). My God, who is sufficient for these things?"

Phillips Brooks used to counsel young preachers with these words: "Never allow yourself to feel equal to your work. If you ever find that spirit growing on you, be afraid."[1] And one reason to be afraid is because your Father will break you and humble you. Is there any reason to think that God should fit you for the ministry of preaching any differently than he did Paul?

> We were so utterly burdened beyond our strength that we despaired of life itself. Indeed, we felt that we had received the sentence of death. But that was to make us rely not on ourselves but on God who raises the dead. (1:8–9)

> To keep me from becoming conceited because of the surpassing greatness of the revelations, a thorn was given me in the flesh . . . to keep me from becoming conceited. (12:7)

The dangers of self-reliance and self-exaltation in the ministry of preaching are so insidious that God will strike us if he must in order to break us of our self-assurance and our casual use of professional techniques.

So Paul rose to preach (he says in 1 Cor. 2:3) "in weakness and in fear and much trembling"—reverent before the glory of the Lord, broken in his native pride, crucified with Christ, shunning the airs of eloquence and intellect. And what happened? There was a demonstration of the Spirit and power (2:4)!

Without this demonstration of Spirit and power in our preaching, nothing of any abiding value will be achieved no matter how many people may admire our cogency or enjoy our illustrations or learn from our doctrine. The goal of preaching is the glory of God in the glad submission of his people. How is God to get the glory from an act that is so manifestly human? First Peter 4:10–11 gives a resounding answer to that question:

> As each has received a gift, use it to serve one another, as good stewards of God's varied grace: whoever speaks, as one who speaks oracles of God; whoever serves, as one who serves by the strength that God supplies—in order that in everything God may be glorified through Jesus Christ. To him belong glory and dominion forever and ever. Amen.

In other words, Peter says, when it comes to speaking and serving, speak the oracles of God in reliance on the *power* of God, and the result will be the *glory* of God. Or to put it another way, in preaching, the one who sets the agenda and gives the power gets the glory. So if the goal of preaching is to be attained, we simply must preach the Word inspired by the Spirit of God in the power given by the Spirit of God.

So let's focus on these two aspects of preaching—the oracles of God that the Spirit has inspired and the power of God brought to us in the anointing of his Spirit. Unless we learn how to rely on the Word of the Spirit and the power of the Spirit in all lowliness and meekness, it is not God who will get the glory in our preaching.

1. Relying on the Gift of the Spirit's Word—the Bible

Oh, how much there is that needs to be said about the use of the Bible in preaching! Relying on the Holy Spirit at this point means believing heartily that "all Scripture is breathed out by God and profitable for teaching, for reproof, for correction, and for training in righteousness" (2 Tim. 3:16). It means believing that "no prophecy [which in the context of 2 Pet. 1:19 means *Scripture*] was ever produced by the will of man, but men spoke from God as they were carried along by the Holy Spirit" (2 Pet. 1:21). It means having strong confidence that the words of Scripture are "not taught by human wisdom but taught by the Spirit" (1 Cor. 2:13). Where the Bible is esteemed as the inspired and inerrant Word of God, preaching can flourish. But where the Bible is treated as a record of valuable religious insight, preaching dies.

But it is not automatic that preaching will flourish where the Bible is believed to be inerrant. Among evangelicals today there are other very effective ways of undercutting the power and authority of biblical preaching. There are subjectivist epistemologies that belittle propositional revelation. There are linguistic theories that cultivate an exegetical atmosphere of ambiguity. And there is a kind of popular, cultural relativism that enables people to dispense flippantly with uncomfortable biblical teaching.

Where these kinds of things take root, the Bible will be silenced in the church, and preaching will become a reflection of current issues and religious opinions. Surely this is not what Paul meant when he said to Timothy, "I charge you in the presence of God and of Christ Jesus, who is to judge the living and the dead, and by his appearing and his kingdom: preach the word!" (2 Tim. 4:1–2). *The Word!* There's the focus. All Christian preaching should be the exposition and application of biblical texts. Our authority as preachers sent by God rises and falls with our manifest allegiance to the text of Scripture. I say *manifest* because there are so many preachers who say they are doing exposition when they do not ground their assertions explicitly—"manifestly"—in the text. They don't show their people clearly that the assertions of their preaching are coming from specific readable words of Scripture that the people can see for themselves.

One of the biggest problems I have with younger preachers whom I am called on to critique is to get them to quote the parts of the text that support the points they are making. It makes me wonder if they have been taught that you should get the drift of a text and then talk in your own words for thirty minutes. The effect of that kind of preaching is to leave people groping for the Word of God and wondering whether what you said is really in the Bible.

Instead, in the literate Western culture we need to get people to open their Bibles and put their finger on the text.[2] Then we need to quote a piece of our text and explain what it means. Tell them which half of the verse it is in. People lose the whole drift of a message groping for where the pastor's ideas are coming from. Then we should quote another piece of the text and explain what it means. Our explanation will draw in other passages of Scripture. Quote them! Don't say general things like, "As Jesus says in the Sermon on the Mount." And along the way or at the end we should urge it into their consciences with penetrating application.

We are simply pulling rank on people when we tell them and don't show them from the text. This does not honor the Word of God or the work of the Holy Spirit. I urge you to rely on the Holy Spirit by saturating your preaching with the Word that he inspired.

We should also rely on the Holy Spirit for help in interpreting the Word. Paul said in 1 Corinthians 2:13–14 that he is "interpreting spiritual truths to those who are spiritual [that is, those who possess the Spirit]. The natural person does not accept the things of the Spirit of God, for they are folly to him." In other words, it takes the Holy Spirit to make us docile to the Bible. The work of the Holy Spirit in the process of interpretation is not to add information, but to give us the discipline to study well, and the humility to accept the truth we find without twisting it, and often a desperately needed discovery or insight in his providential guidance of our work.

I urge you to be like John Wesley in this matter of relying on the Spirit in his Word, the Bible. He said, "O give me that book! At any price give me the book of God! I have it: here is knowledge enough for me. Let me be a man of one book."[3]

It is not that reading other books or knowing the contemporary world is unimportant, but the greater danger is to neglect the study of the Bible. When you finish seminary and are in the church ministry, there are no courses, no assignments, no teachers to make you study. Just you and your Bible and your books. And the vast majority of preachers fall far short of the resolution that Jonathan Edwards made when he was in his twenties: "*Resolved*, To study the Scriptures so steadily, constantly, and frequently, as that I may find, and plainly perceive, myself to grow in the knowledge of the same."[4]

The really effective preachers have been ever-growing in the Word of God. Their delight is in the law of the Lord and on his law they meditate day and night (Ps. 1:2). Spurgeon said of John Bunyan, "Prick him anywhere; and you will find that his blood is Bibline, the very essence of the Bible flows from him. He cannot speak without quoting a text, for his soul is full of the Word of God."[5] And ours should be too. That is what it means to rely on the gift of the Spirit's Word.

2. Relying on the Gift of the Spirit's Power in Preaching

We turn now finally to the actual experience of the Spirit's power in the event of preaching. First Peter 4:11 says, "Whoever serves . . . [let him serve] by the strength that God supplies—in order that in everything God may be glorified through Jesus Christ." The one who gives the power gets the glory. How do you preach like this? Practically what does it mean to do something—like preaching—in another person's power?

Paul said something similar in 1 Corinthians 15:10: "I worked harder than any of them, though it was not I, but the grace of God that is with me." And in Romans 15:18 he said, "I will not venture to speak of anything except what Christ has accomplished through me to bring the Gentiles to obedience—by word and deed." How do you preach so that the preaching is a demonstration of God's power and not your own?

I am ever learning the answer to that question in my own life and preaching. After more than two decades of weekly preaching, I often feel like a beginner. So for me to say, "Here is how you preach in the power of the Holy Spirit," is a very risky thing. What I would like to do is tell you where I am in the quest for this precious and indispensable experience of the Spirit.

There are five steps that I follow in seeking to preach not in my own strength but in the strength that God supplies. I sum them up with an acronym so that I can remember them when my mind is befogged by fear or distraction. The acronym is *APTAT.*

Picture me in the front pew at Bethlehem Baptist Church. Two minutes remain before I stand to preach. One of the elders or an apprentice steps to the pulpit to read the text for the morning message before I come. As he begins to read, I bow my head before the Lord for one last transaction before the sacred moment of preaching. I almost always put my heart through *APTAT* before the Lord.

1. I *Admit* to the Lord that without him I can do nothing. I affirm that John 15:5 is absolutely true of me at this moment: "Apart from me you can do nothing." I admit to God: My heart would not beat without you. My eyes could not see without

you. My memory would fail without you. Without you I will be plagued with distraction and self-consciousness. Without you I will doubt your reality. Without you I will not love the people. Without you I will feel no awe at the truth I am about to speak. Without you the Word will fall on deaf ears. Who but you can raise the dead? Without you, O God, I can do nothing.

2. Therefore, Father, I *Pray* for help. I beg for the insight and the power and the humility and the love and the memory and the freedom that I need to preach this message for the glory of your name and the gladness of your people and the ingathering of your elect. I accept your invitation, "Call upon me in the day of trouble; I will deliver you, and you shall glorify me" (Ps. 50:15).

And I should perhaps mention that this is not the beginning of my prayer for this sermon. Its preparation was done in almost constant prayer for help, and I get up three and a half hours before the first service to spend two hours getting my heart as ready as I can before I come to the church. And during that time I search for a promise in the Word that will be the basis of the next step in APTAT in those last minutes.

3. The next step is *Trust*—not merely in a general way in God's goodness, but in a specific promise where I can bank my hope for that hour. I find this kind of specific trust in a particular Word of God utterly essential to fight off the assault of Satan in those moments. Recently I strengthened myself with Psalm 40:17: "As for me, I am poor and needy, but the Lord takes thought for me. You are my help and my deliverer; do not delay, O my God!" I memorize the verse early in the morning, recite it to myself in that moment, believe it, resist the devil with it, and . . .

4. I *Act* in the confidence that God will fulfill his Word. And I can testify that, though the fullness of blessings that I long to see has been delayed. God has met me and my people again in the display of his glory and the glad submission of his people. This leads up to the final step.

5. I *Thank* God at the end of the message that I was sustained and that the truth of his Word and the purchase of his cross have been preached in some measure in the power of his Spirit to the glory of his name.

And I dream that in twenty years some forty-two-year-old preacher will stand in his pulpit with a ministry a hundred times as fruitful as mine and say, "John Piper never knew it, but when I sat under his preaching, the glory of God and the cross of Christ and the power of the Spirit were irresistible, and God called me to the ministry of the Word."

4

The Gravity and Gladness
of Preaching

TWO HUNDRED AND FIFTY years ago Jonathan Edwards's preaching sparked a great awakening among the churches. He was a great theologian (some would say, second to none in church history), a great man of God, and a great preacher. We can't copy him uncritically, but oh, what we could learn from this man, especially about the weighty business of preaching!

From the time he was a young man he was overwhelmingly earnest and intense in all that he did. One of his college resolutions was, "*Resolved,* to live with all my might while I do live."[1] His preaching was totally serious from beginning to end. You will look in vain for one joke in the twelve hundred sermons that remain. He preached an ordination sermon in 1744 and said:

> If a minister has light without heat, and entertains his [hearers] with learned discourses, without a savour of the power of godliness, or any appearance of fervency of spirit, and zeal for God

and the good of souls, he may gratify itching ears, and fill the heads of his people with empty notions; but it will not be very likely to teach their hearts, or save their souls.[2]

Edwards had an overwhelming conviction of the reality of the glories of heaven and horrors of hell that made his preaching utterly earnest. He came under severe criticism for his participation in the revival fervor. The Boston clergy, like Charles Chauncy, accused him and others of stirring up far too much emotion with their dreadful seriousness about eternity. In 1741 Edwards responded like this:

> If any of you that are heads of families, saw one of your children in a house that was all on fire over its head, and in imminent danger of being soon consumed in the flames, that seemed to be very insensible of its danger, and neglected to escape, after you had often spake to it, and called to it, would you go on to speak to it only in a cold and indifferent manner? Would not you cry aloud, and call earnestly to it, and represent the danger it was in, and its own folly in delaying, in the most lively manner you were capable of? Would not nature itself teach this, and oblige you to it? If you should continue to speak to it only in a cold manner, as you are wont to do in ordinary conversation about indifferent matters, would not those about you begin to think you were bereft of reason yourself? . . .
>
> If [then] we who have the care of souls, knew what hell was, had seen the state of the damned, or by any other means, become sensible how dreadful their case was . . . and saw our hearers in imminent danger, and that they were not sensible of their danger . . . it would be morally impossible for us to avoid abundantly

and most earnestly setting before them the dreadfulness of that misery they were in danger of . . . and warning them to fly from it, and even to cry aloud to them.[3]

From the testimonies of his contemporaries we know that Edwards's sermons were tremendously powerful in their effect on the people in his Northampton congregation. Why was this? It was not because he was anything like the dramatic orator that George Whitefield was. In the days of the awakening he still wrote his sermons out in full and read them, by and large, without gesture.

Then where was his power? Sereno Dwight, who assembled Edwards's memoirs, said:

One of the positive causes of his . . . great success as a preacher, was the deep and pervading solemnity of his mind. He had, at all times, a solemn consciousness of the presence of God. This was visible in his looks and his demeanor. It obviously had a controlling influence over all his preparations for the pulpit; and was most manifest in all his public services. Its effect on the audience was immediate and not to be resisted.[4]

Dwight asked a man who had heard Edwards personally whether he was an eloquent preacher. The man said:

He had no studied varieties of the voice, and no strong emphasis. He scarcely gestured, or even moved; and he made no attempt by the elegance of his style, or the beauty of his pictures, to gratify the taste, and fascinate the imagination. But, if you mean by eloquence, the power of presenting an important truth before an audience, with overwhelming weight of argument, and with such intenseness of feeling, that the whole soul of the speaker is thrown into every part of the conception and delivery; so that the solemn attention of the whole audience is riveted, from the beginning to the close, and impressions are left that cannot be effaced; Mr. Edwards was the most eloquent man I ever heard speak.[5]

Intensity of feeling, the weight of argument, a deep and pervading solemnity of mind, a savor of the power of godliness, fervency of spirit, zeal for God—these are the marks of the "gravity of preaching." If there is one thing we can learn from Jonathan Edwards, it is to take our calling seriously, not to trifle with the Word of God and the act of preaching.

A hundred years after Edwards a hypocritical pastor named Thomas Chalmers got converted in his little parish of Kilmany. He became a powerful force for evangelicalism and for world missions from his pastorate in Glasgow and from his lectern at the University of St. Andrews and then Edinburgh. His fame and power in the pulpit were legendary in his lifetime.

But why? James Stewart describes his preaching like this: "He preached with a disconcertingly provincial accent, with an almost total lack of dramatic gesture, tied rigidly to his manuscript, with his finger following the written lines as he read."[6] Andrew Blackwood refers to Chalmers's "bondage to the manuscript and use of long sentences."[7] What then was his secret? James Alexander, who was teaching at Princeton at that time, asked John Mason on his return from Scotland why Chalmers was so effective, and Mason replied, "It is his blood-earnestness."[8]

I want to give as strong a conviction as words can convey that the work of preaching is to be done in *blood-earnestness*. We are in no danger today of mechanical imitation of Edwards and Chalmers and their Puritan fathers. We have fallen so far from their conception of preaching that we couldn't imitate it if we tried. I say *fallen* because, whether a manuscript should be read or not, and whether a sermon should be two hours or not, and whether sentences should be long and stories few, the fact is that the glory of these preachers was their earnestness—an earnestness that might be called gravity. From that we have fallen so far that we can scarcely find positive categories to describe the atmosphere of this old preaching. Most people today have so little experience of deep, earnest, reverent, powerful encounters with God in preaching that the only associations that come to mind when the notion is mentioned are that the preacher is morose or boring or dismal or sullen or gloomy or surly or unfriendly.

If you endeavor to bring a holy hush upon your people in a worship service, you can be assured that someone will say that the atmosphere is unfriendly or cold. All that many people can imagine is that the absence of chatter would mean the presence of stiffness and awkwardness and unfriendliness. Since they have little or no experience of the deep gladness of momentous moments of gravity, they strive for gladness the only way they know how—by being lighthearted and chipper and talkative.

Pastors have absorbed this narrow view of gladness and friendliness and now cultivate it across the land with pulpit demeanor and verbal casualness that make the blood-earnestness of Chalmers and the pervading solemnity of Edwards's mind unthinkable. The result is a preaching atmosphere and a preaching style plagued by triviality, levity, carelessness, flippancy, and a general spirit that nothing of eternal and infinite proportions is being done or said on Sunday morning.

If I were to put my thesis into a measured sentence it would go like this: *Gladness and gravity should be woven together in the life and preaching of a pastor in such a way as to sober the careless soul and sweeten the burdens of the saints.* I say *sweeten* because it connotes some of the poignancy of the gladness I have in mind, and sets it off from the glib and petty attempts to stir up lightheartedness in a congregation.

Another way to say it would be this: Love for people does not take precious realities lightly (hence the call for the gravity of preaching), and love for people does not load people with the burden of obedience without providing the strength of joy to help them carry it (hence the call for the gladness of preaching).

Let me dwell for a moment on the necessity of gladness in preaching as an act of love. It continually amazes people when I say that if a pastor is to truly love his people he must diligently pursue his happiness in the ministry of the Word. People have been taught consistently that to be a loving person you must abandon the pursuit of your own joy. It's all right to get it as an unexpected and unpursued result of love (as if that were psychologically possible), but it is not all right to pursue your happiness.

I assert the opposite: If you are indifferent to your joy in ministry, you are indifferent to an essential element of love. And if you try to abandon your joy in the ministry of the Word, you strive against God and your people. Consider Hebrews 13:17.

Obey your leaders and submit to them, for they are keeping watch over your souls, as those who will have to give account. Let them do this with joy (*meta charas*) and not with groaning (*stenazontes*), for that would be of no advantage to you (*alusiteles gar humin touto*).

A pastor who reads this cannot come away indifferent to his joy if he loves his people. The text says that joyless ministry is no advantage to a people. But love aims at the advantage of our people. Therefore, love cannot neglect the cultivation of its own joy in the ministry of the Word. Peter puts it in the form of a command: "Shepherd the flock of God that is among you . . . not under compulsion, but willingly . . . not for shameful gain, but eagerly" (1 Pet. 5:2–3). *Willingly* and *eagerly* are just different words for *gladly*.

One reason an essential element of love is the enjoyment of our work of preaching is that you can't consistently give what you don't have. And if you don't give gladness, you don't give the gospel; you give legalism. A pastor who guts out his work in gladless "obedience" transmits that kind of life to his people, and the name of it is hypocrisy and legalistic bondage, not the freedom of those whose yoke is easy and whose burden is light.

Another answer is that a pastor who is not manifestly glad in God does not glorify God. He cannot make God look glorious if knowing and serving this God gives no gladness to his soul. A bored and unenthusiastic tour guide in the Alps contradicts and dishonors the majesty of the mountains.

So Phillips Brooks was right when he said a hundred years ago:

> It is essential to the preacher's success that he should thoroughly enjoy his work. . . . Its highest joy is in the great ambition that is set before it, the glorifying of the Lord and the saving of the souls of men. No other joy on earth compares with that. . . . As we read the lives of all the most effective preachers of the past, or as we meet the men who are powerful preachers of the Word today, we feel how certainly and how deeply the very exercise of their ministry delights them.[9]

The gladness of preaching is biblically essential if we would love men and glorify God—and these are the two great ends of preaching!

But what a difference there is between the joy of Jonathan Edwards and the smiles and jokes of so many pastors! And at least part of the reason is that the strands of their happiness are not woven together with a holy gravity. Edwards said:

> All gracious affections, that are a sweet odor to Christ, and that fill the soul of a Christian with a heavenly sweetness and fragrancy, are brokenhearted affections. . . . The desires of the saints, however earnest, are humble desires: their hope is a humble hope; their joy, even when it is unspeakable, and full of glory, is a humble, brokenhearted joy.[10]

There is something about the sheer weight of our sinfulness and the magnitude of God's holiness and the momentousness of our calling that should give a fragrance of humble gravity to the gladness of our preaching.

Why? Why this stress on gravity, especially if gladness is so essential? Let me mention the reason and then conclude with some suggestions on how to cultivate the interweaving of gladness and gravity that I am trying to describe.

Gravity in preaching is appropriate because preaching is God's appointed means for the conversion of sinners, the awakening of the church, and the preservation of the saints. If preaching fails in its task, the consequences are infinitely terrible. "Since, in the wisdom of God, the world did not know God through wisdom, it pleased God through the folly of what we preach to save those who believe" (1 Cor. 1:21).

God saves people from everlasting ruin through preaching. When Paul ponders this in 2 Corinthians 2:15–16 he feels the overwhelming weight of this responsibility: "We are the aroma of Christ to God among those who are being saved and among those who are perishing, to one a fragrance from death to death, to the other a fragrance from life to life. Who is sufficient for these things?"

This is simply stupendous to think about—that when I preach, the everlasting destiny of sinners hangs in the balance! If a person is not made earnest and grave by this fact, people will unconsciously learn that the realities of heaven and hell are not serious. And I can't help but think that this is what is being communicated by the casual cleverness that comes from so many pulpits. James Denney said, "No man can give the impression that he himself is clever and that Christ is mighty to save."[11] John Henry Jowett said, "We never reach the innermost room in any man's soul by the expediencies of the showman or the buffoon."[12] And yet today it seems to be the stock in trade of many preachers that they must say something cute or clever or funny.

There actually seems to be a fear of approaching Chalmers's *blood-earnestness.* I have seen a strange silence begin to come over a congregation and watched the preacher, seemingly intentionally, dispel it quickly with some lighthearted quip or the use of a pun or a witticism.

Laughter seems to have replaced repentance as the goal of many preachers. Laughter means people feel good. It means they like you. It means you have moved them. It means you have some measure of power. It seems to have all the marks of successful communication—if the depth of sin and the holiness of God and the danger of hell and need for broken hearts are left out of account.

I have been amazed at conferences where preachers mention the need for revival and then proceed to cultivate an atmosphere in which it could never come. In the early years of my ministry I read *Lectures on Revivals* by William Sprague and the memoirs of Asahel Nettleton, a powerful evangelist in the Second Great Awakening who worked the same time Charles Finney did. What I learned there is that deep and abiding spiritual awakening is attended by a Spirit-given seriousness among the people of God. Some lines from Nettleton's *Memoirs*:

> Fall of 1812, South Salem, Connecticut: "His preaching pro-
> duced an immediate solemnity on the minds of the people. . . .
> The seriousness soon spread through the place, and the subject
> of religion became the engrossing topic of conversation." Spring
> of 1813, North Lyme: "There was no special seriousness when
> he commenced his labors. But a deep solemnity soon pervaded
> the congregation." August, 1814, East Granby: "The effect of
> his entrance into the place was electric. The schoolhouse . . . was
> filled with trembling worshippers. A solemnity and seriousness
> pervaded the community."[13]

The very first thing Sprague mentions in his chapter on the means of producing and promoting revivals is *seriousness*.

> I appeal to any of you who have been in the midst of a revival,
> whether a deep solemnity did not pervade the scene. . . . And
> if you at such a moment have wished to be gay, have you not
> felt that that was not the place for it? . . . It were worse than
> preposterous to think of carrying forward such a work by any
> means which are not marked by the deepest seriousness, or

to introduce any thing which is adapted to awaken and cherish the lighter emotions, when all such emotions should be awed out of the mind. All ludicrous anecdotes, and modes of expression, and gestures, and attitudes, are never more out of place than when the Holy Spirit is moving upon the hearts of a congregation. Every thing of this kind is fitted to grieve him away; because it directly contradicts the errand on which he has come;—that of convincing sinners of their guilt, and renewing them to repentance.[14]

In spite of this historical reality that seems so obvious from the very nature of things, even preachers that bemoan the absence of revival in our day seem locked into a cavalier demeanor in front of a group of people. Sometimes it seems that levity is the greatest enemy of any true spiritual work being done in the hearers.

Charles Spurgeon had a deep and robust sense of humor. He could use it for great effect. Some, when reading his sermons, have thought him funny. But Robertson Nicoll wrote about Spurgeon three years after his death:

Evangelism of the humorous type may attract multitudes but it lays the soul in ashes and destroys the very germs of religion. Mr. Spurgeon is thought by those who do not know his sermons to have been a humorous preacher. As a matter of fact there was no preacher whose tone was more uniformly earnest, reverent and solemn.[15]

Spurgeon is an especially helpful example because he believed so deeply in the proper place of humor and laughter. He said to his students:

We must conquer—some of us especially—our tendency to levity. A great distinction exists between holy cheerfulness, which is a virtue, and that general levity, which is a vice. There is a levity which has not enough heart to laugh, but trifles with everything; it is flippant, hollow, unreal. A hearty laugh is no more levity than a hearty cry.[16]

And surely it is a sign of the age that we preachers are far more adept at humor than tears. The apostle Paul spoke of sinners in Philippians 3:18–19 like this: "Many, of whom I have often told you and now tell you even with tears, walk as enemies of the cross of Christ. Their end is destruction . . . with minds set on earthly things." Without that weeping there will never be the revival we need, nor deep and lasting spiritual renewal.

Would there not come upon a congregation a powerful spirit of love and conviction if a pastor, with all earnestness and gravity, could begin his Easter sermon not with a joke or a cute story, but with the words of John Donne to his congregation:

What Sea could furnish my eyes with tears enough to pour out, if I should think, that of all this congregation, which looks me in the face now, I should not meet one at the Resurrection, at that right hand of God![17]

Gravity and earnestness in our preaching are appropriate not only (as we have seen) because preaching is God's instrument for the weighty business of saving sinners and reviving his church, but also because it is God's instrument for preserving the saints. Paul says in 2 Timothy 2:10, "I endure everything for the sake of the elect, that they also may obtain the salvation that is in Christ Jesus with eternal glory." In other words, labor on behalf of the elect is not icing on the cake of their eternal security. It is God's appointed means of keeping them secure. Eternal security is a community project (Heb. 3:12–13), and preaching is part of God's securing power. He calls effectually by the Word and he keeps effectually by the Word.

There is a mechanical view of eternal security that drains the blood-earnestness right out of the weekly ministry of preaching to the saints. But biblically, the perseverance of the saints hangs on the earnest application of the means of grace, and one of those means is the preaching of God's Word. Heaven and hell are at stake every Sunday morning, not merely because unbelievers might be present, but also because our people are saved "*if* indeed [they] continue in the faith" (Col. 1:23), and faith comes—and stays—by the hearing of the Word of God in the gospel (Rom. 10:17).

Surely every preacher should say, with all gravity, "Who is sufficient for these things"—to save sinners, to revive the church, to preserve the saints! So I repeat my thesis: *Gladness and gravity should be woven together in the life and preaching of a pastor in such a way as to sober the careless soul and sweeten the burdens of the saints.* Love for people cannot treat awesome realities lightly (hence, gravity!), and love for people cannot load people with the burden of joyless obedience (hence, gladness!).

I close with seven practical suggestions for cultivating this gravity and gladness in your preaching.

1. *Strive for practical, earnest, glad-hearted holiness in every area of your life.* I mentioned earlier that when Robert Murray M'Cheyne was a pastor he said that what his people needed more than anything else was his personal holiness. One of the reasons is that you can't be something in the pulpit that you aren't during the week—

at least not for long! You can't be blood-earnest in the pulpit and habitually flippant at the board meeting and the church dinner. Nor can you display the glory of God in the gladness of your preaching if you are surly and dismal and unfriendly during the week. Don't strive to be a kind of preacher. Strive to be a kind of person!

2. *Make your life—especially the life of your study—a life of constant communion with God in prayer.* The aroma of God will not linger on a person who does not linger in the presence of God. Richard Cecil said that "the leading defect in Christian Ministers was the want of a devotional habit."[18] We are called to the ministry of the word *and prayer,* because without prayer the God of our studies will be the unfrightening and uninspiring God of insipid academic gamesmanship.

Fruitful study and fervent prayer live and die together. B. B. Warfield once heard a person say that ten minutes on your knees will give you a truer, deeper knowledge of God than ten hours over your books. His response was exactly right: "What! than ten hours over your books on your knees?"[19] And the same should be true in the actual preparation of our sermons. Cotton Mather's rule was to stop at the end of every paragraph as he wrote his sermon to pray and examine himself and try to fix on his heart some holy impression of his subject.[20] Without this spirit of constant prayer, we cannot maintain the gravity and gladness that lingers in the vicinity of the throne of grace.

3. *Read books that were written by men or women who bleed Bible when you prick them and who are blood-earnest about the truths they discuss.* In fact I found it to be life-changing advice when a wise seminary professor told us to find one great evangelical theologian and immerse ourselves in his life and writing. I can scarcely overstate the effect it has had on my life to live with Jonathan Edwards month in and month out since my seminary days. And through him to find

my way into the most earnest men in the world—Calvin, Luther, Bunyan, Burroughs, Bridges, Flavel, Owen, Charnock, Gurnall, Watson, Sibbes, Ryle! Find the books that are blood-earnest about God and you will discover they know the path that leads to joy more accurately than many contemporary guides.

4. *Direct your mind often to the contemplation of death.* It is absolutely inevitable if the Lord tarries, and it is utterly momentous. Not to think on its implications for life and preaching is incredibly naïve. Edwards was the man he was—with depth and power (and eleven believing children!)—because of resolutions like these that he made as a young man:

9. *Resolved,* To think much, on all occasions, of my dying, and of the common circumstances which attend death.

55. *Resolved,* To endeavor to my utmost, so to act, as I can think I should do, if I had already seen the happiness of heaven and torments of hell.[21]

Every funeral I perform is a deeply sobering experience for me because I sit there before my message and imagine myself or my wife or sons or daughter in that coffin. Death and sickness have an amazing way of blowing the haze of triviality out of life and replacing it with the wisdom of gravity and gladness in the hope of resurrection joy.

5. *Consider the biblical teaching that as a preacher you will be judged with greater strictness.* "Not many of you should become teachers, my brothers, for you know that we who teach will be judged with greater strictness" (James 3:1). The writer of Hebrews says of pastors, "They are keeping watch over your souls, as those who will have to

give an account" (Heb. 13:17). And Paul puts it most ominously in Acts 20 when he says to the people that he has been teaching in Ephesus, "I am innocent of the blood of all, for I did not shrink from declaring to you the whole counsel of God" (Acts 20:26–27). Evidently, not to teach God's counsel with fullness and faithfulness can leave the blood of our people on our hands. If we consider these things as we should, the gravity of the responsibility and the gladness of its successful outcome will shape everything we do.

6. *Consider the example of Jesus.* He was as kind and tender and gentle as a righteous man could be. He was not morose. They said John the Baptist had a demon, but they said Jesus was a glutton and a drunkard, a friend of tax collectors and sinners. He was not a psychopathic killjoy. But he was a man of sorrows and acquainted with grief. He never preached a careless sermon, and there is no record of a careless word. He never told a joke that we know of, and all his humor was a sheath for the blood-earnest rapier of truth. Jesus is the great example for preachers—the crowds heard him gladly, the children sat in his lap, the women were honored, and no one in the Bible spoke of hell more often or in more horrible terms.

7. *Finally, strive with all the strength you have to know God and to humble yourself under his mighty hand* (1 Pet. 5:6). Don't be content to guide people among the foothills of his glory. Become a mountain climber on the cliffs of God's majesty. And let the truth begin to overwhelm you that you will never exhaust the heights of God. Every time you climb over a rim of insight there stretches out before you, disappearing into the clouds, a thousand miles of massive beauty in the character of God. Set yourself to climb, and ponder the thought that everlasting ages of discovery in the infinite Being of God will not suffice to weaken your gladness in the glory of God or dull the intensity of gravity in his presence.

PART 2

———

HOW TO MAKE GOD SUPREME IN PREACHING

Guidance from the Ministry of Jonathan Edwards

WHEN I WAS IN SEMINARY, a wise professor told me that, in addition to reading the Bible, I ought to choose one great theologian and apply myself throughout life to understanding and mastering his thought—to sink at least one shaft deep into reality rather than always dabbling on the surface of things. I might, in time, be able to "converse" with this man as a kind of peer, and know at least one system with which to bring other ideas into fruitful dialogue. It was good advice.

The theologian I have devoted myself to is Jonathan Edwards. I owe him more than I can ever explain. He has fed my soul with the beauty of God and holiness and heaven when every other door seemed closed to me. He has renewed my hope and my vision for ministry in some very low times. He has opened the window on the world of the Spirit time and again when all I could see were curtains of secularism. He has shown me the possibility of mingling rigorous thought about God and warm affection for God. He embodies the truth that theology exists for doxology. He could spend whole mornings in ejaculatory prayer walking in the woods outside Northampton. He had a passion for truth and a passion for lost sinners. All of this flourished in the pastorate. Above all, Edwards was a God-besotted preacher. And that is why he is so important in a book on the supremacy of God in preaching.

Jonathan Edwards preached the way he did because of the man he was and the God he saw. The following chapters will deal in turn with Edwards's life, theology, and preaching.

5

Keep God Central

The Life of Jonathan Edwards

JONATHAN EDWARDS WAS BORN in 1703 in Windsor, Connecticut.[1] His father was the local pastor, and taught his only son Latin when he turned six. At twelve little Edwards was sent off to Yale. And five years later he graduated with highest honors and gave the valedictory address in Latin. He studied for the ministry for two more years at Yale, then took a brief pastorate at a Presbyterian church in New York. Beginning in 1723, Edwards tutored at Yale for three years. Then came the call to the Congregational church of Northampton, Massachusetts. Edwards's grandfather, Solomon Stoddard, had been pastor there for over half a century. He handpicked Edwards as his apprentice and successor. The partnership began in February 1727. Stoddard died in 1729. Edwards remained the pastor until 1750—a twenty-three-year relationship.

Back in 1723 Edwards had fallen in love with a thirteen-year-old girl named Sarah Pierrepont who proved to be just the kind of woman who could share his religious transport. On the front page of his Greek grammar he wrote the only kind of love song of which his heart was capable:

> They say there is a young lady in [New Haven] who is loved of that Great Being who made and rules the world. . . . She will sometimes go about from place to place, singing sweetly, and seems to be always full of joy and pleasure; and no one knows for what. She loves to be alone walking in the fields and groves, and seems to have someone invisible always conversing with her.[2]

Four years later, five months after his installation at Northampton, they were married. They had eleven children (eight daughters and three sons), all of whom revered their father and brought no reproach upon the family, in spite of having a father who spent as many as thirteen hours a day studying.

For better or worse, Edwards did not practice regular pastoral visitation among his people (620 communicants in 1735). He went if sent for by the sick. He preached frequently at private meetings in particular neighborhoods. He catechized the children. And he encouraged anyone under religious conviction to come to him in his study for counsel. His own judgment about himself was that he was not a gifted conversationalist and that he could do the greatest good to the souls of men, and most promote the cause of Christ, by preaching and writing.[3] At least during the early years of his Northampton pastorate Edwards preached two sermons a week, one on Sunday and one on a weekday evening. Sermons in those days were generally an hour in length, but could last considerably longer.

When he was still in college Edwards had written seventy resolutions. We saw already the one which says, "*Resolved,* to live with all my might while I do live."[4] For him that came to mean a passionate devotion to the study of divinity. He maintained an extremely rigorous study schedule. He said that he thought "Christ commended rising early in the morning by his rising from the grave very early."[5] So he rose generally between four and five to enter his study. He would always study with pen in hand, thinking out every insight and recording it in his countless notebooks. Even on his travels he would pin pieces of paper to his coat to remind himself of insights he had along the way.

In the evening, when most pastors are either exhausted on the couch or at a finance committee meeting, Edwards returned to his study after spending an hour with his children after dinner. There were exceptions. On January 22, 1734, he wrote in his diary, "I judge that it is best, when I am in a good frame for divine contemplation . . . that, ordinarily, I will not be interrupted by going to dinner, but will forego my dinner, rather than be broke off."[6]

That may sound unhealthy, especially for one whose six-foot-one-inch frame was never robust. But as a matter of fact, Edwards watched his diet and his exercise with great care. Everything was calculated to optimize his efficiency and power in study. He abstained from every quantity and kind of food that made him sick or sleepy. In the winter he got his exercise by chopping firewood, and in the summer he would ride horseback and walk in the fields.

Regarding these walks in the fields he once wrote, "Sometimes on fair days I find myself more particularly disposed to regard the glories of the world than to betake myself to the study of serious religion."[7] So he had his struggles too. But for Edwards it wasn't a struggle between nature and God, but between two different experiences of God:

Once as I rode out into the woods for my health in 1737, having alighted from my horse in a retired place, as my manner commonly has been, to walk for divine contemplation and prayer, I had a view, that for me was extraordinary, of the glory of the Son of God, as Mediator between God and man, and his wonderful, great, full, pure and sweet grace and love and meek, gentle condescension . . . which continued, as near as I can judge, about an hour; which kept me the greater part of the time in a flood of tears, and weeping aloud.[8]

He had an extraordinary love for the glory of God in nature. The good effects of this love on his capacity to delight in the greatness of God and on the imagery of his preaching were tremendous.

Edwards committed some pastoral blunders that lit the fuse that eventually exploded in his dismissal from his church. For example, in 1744 he implicated some innocent young people in an obscenity scandal. But what ended his pastorate was Edwards's public repudiation of the longstanding tradition in New England that profession of saving faith was not required in order to be a communicant at the Lord's Supper. His grandfather had long defended the practice of admitting people to the Lord's Supper who did not give profession or evidence of having been regenerated. Stoddard saw the Supper as a converting ordinance. Edwards came to reject this as unbiblical and wrote a book to defend his case. But on Friday, June 22, 1750, the decision of dismissal was read, and on July 1 Edwards delivered his "Farewell Sermon." He was forty-six years old and had served the church for half his life.

During all those years he had been the primary human spark plug for the divine voltage that caused the Great Awakening in New

England. There were unusual seasons of revival, especially in the years 1734–35 and 1740–42. Almost all of Edwards's published works during his Northampton days were devoted to interpreting, defending, and promoting what he believed was a surprising work of God and no mere emotional hysteria.

This should help us keep in mind that Edwards's preaching generally had a wider audience than his own parish. He always had in mind Christ's Kingdom on earth, and he knew his voice was reverberating beyond the borders of Northampton. Some of his works were published in Britain before they were published in Boston.

After his dismissal from Northampton, he accepted a call to Stockbridge in western Massachusetts as pastor of the church there and missionary to the Indians. He worked there until 1758, when he went to be president of Princeton.

These seven years in out-of-the-way Stockbridge were immensely productive years for Edwards, and in 1757 he was just starting to feel at home. So on October 19, 1757, after being called to the presidency of Princeton, Edwards wrote to the trustees of Princeton, trying to convince them that he was unfit for the job:

> I have a constitution, in many respects, peculiarly unhappy, at-
> tended with flaccid solids, vapid, sizy, and scarce fluids, and a
> low tide of spirits; often occasioning a kind of childish weakness
> and contemptibleness of speech, presence, and demeanor, with a
> disagreeable dulness and stiffness, much unfitting me for conver-
> sation, but more especially for the government of a college. . . . I
> am also deficient in some parts of learning, particularly in algebra,
> and the higher parts of mathematics, and the Greek classics; my
> Greek learning having been chiefly in the New Testament.[9]

One wonders how well he had preserved his Hebrew through thirty years of pastoral labor, because he says that he would never want to spend his time teaching languages, "unless it be the Hebrew tongue; which I should be willing to improve myself in, by instructing others." But what is typical of the man is that at fifty-four he was desirous of improving his grasp of the biblical language. He spoke of the books he planned to write and then pleaded for release to do what his heart longed for: "My heart is so much in these studies, that I cannot find it in my heart to be willing to put myself into an incapacity to pursue them any more in the future part of my life."[10]

So when the council of ministers that Edwards had personally called to Stockbridge voted that it was his duty to accept the presidency, Edwards wept openly before the council but accepted their advice. He left almost immediately and arrived at Princeton in January 1758. On February 13 he was inoculated for small pox with apparent success. But secondary fever set in, large pustules formed on his throat, which prevented his taking medications, and he died on March 22, 1758, at the age of fifty-four.

His last words to the grieving and fearful friends at his bedside were, "Trust in God and ye need not fear."[11] His great trust in the sovereign goodness of God perhaps found its most eloquent expression in the strength of his wife. She received word of her husband's death by letter from his physician. The first response we have record of is the letter she wrote to her daughter Esther on April 3, two weeks after Edwards's death.

My very dear child!

What shall I say? A holy and good God has covered us with a dark cloud. O that we may kiss the rod, and lay our hands on our mouths! The Lord has done it. He has made me adore his goodness, that we had him so long. But my God lives; and he has my heart. O what a legacy my husband, and your father, has left us! We are all given to God; and there I am, and love to be.

Your ever affectionate mother,
Sarah Edwards[12]

6

Submit to Sweet Sovereignty

The Theology of Edwards

WHAT JONATHAN EDWARDS PREACHED and *how* he preached
were owing to his vision of God. So before we discuss his preaching we need a glimpse of that vision. In 1735 Edwards preached a
sermon on the text, "Be still, and know that I am God" (Ps. 46:10).
From the text he develops the following doctrine:

> God doth not require us to submit contrary to reason, but to
> submit as seeing the reason and ground of submission.—Hence,
> the bare consideration that God is God, may well be sufficient
> to still all objections and opposition against the divine sovereign
> dispensations.[1]

When Jonathan Edwards became still and contemplated the
great truth that *God is God,* he saw a majestic Being whose sheer
existence implied infinite power, infinite knowledge, and infinite
holiness. He goes on to argue like this:

It is most evident by the Works of God, that his understanding and power are infinite. . . . Being thus infinite in understanding and power, he must also be perfectly holy; for unholiness always argues some defect, some blindness. Where there is no darkness or delusion, there can be no unholiness. . . . God being infinite in power and knowledge, he must be self-sufficient and all-sufficient; therefore it is impossible that he should be under any temptation to do any thing amiss; for he can have no end in doing it. . . . So God is essentially holy, and nothing is more impossible than that God should do amiss.[2]

For Edwards the infinite power, or absolute sovereignty, of God is the foundation of God's all-sufficiency. And his all-sufficiency is the fountain of his perfect holiness, and his holiness (as Edwards says in *Religious Affections*) comprehends all his moral excellency. So the sovereignty of God for Edwards was utterly crucial to everything else he believed about God.[3]

When he was twenty-six or twenty-seven, he looked back nine years to the time he fell in love with the doctrine of the sovereignty of God and wrote:

There has been a wonderful alteration in my mind, in respect to the doctrine of God's sovereignty, from that day to this. . . . God's absolute sovereignty . . . is what my mind seems to rest assured of, as much as of any thing that I see with my eyes. . . . The doctrine has very often appeared exceeding pleasant, bright, and sweet. Absolute sovereignty is what I love to ascribe to God. . . . God's sovereignty has ever appeared to me, [a] great part of his glory. It has often been my delight to approach God, and adore him as a sovereign God.[4]

So when Edwards beheld God and stood entranced by his absolute sovereignty, he didn't see this reality in isolation. It was part of God's glory. It was sweet to Edwards because it was a great and vital part of an infinitely glorious Person whom he loved with tremendous passion.

Two inferences follow from this vision of God. The first is that *the goal of all that God does is to preserve and display his glory.* All God's actions flow from fullness, not from deficiency. Most of our actions are motivated by the need to make up some deficit or supply some lack in ourselves. God never takes steps to supply his insufficiency. He performs no remedial exercises. As an absolutely sovereign and all-sufficient fountain, all his actions are the overflow of his fullness. To put it differently, he never acts to add to his glory but only to preserve it and display it. (This is unfolded masterfully in Edwards's *Dissertation Concerning the End for Which God Created the World.*[5])

The other inference from his vision of God is that the duty of man is to *delight* in God's glory. I focus on the word *delight* intentionally because many people in Edwards's day and in ours are willing to say that the chief end of man is to glorify God and enjoy him forever. But by and large they consider the enjoyment of God optional and do not understand with Edwards that the chief end of man is to glorify God *by* enjoying him forever.

Delight is what Edwards called an *affection* (we might say emotion). He wrote a great book called *A Treatise Concerning the Religious Affections* in which he wanted to make one main point: "True religion, in great part, consists in holy affections."[6] He defined affections as "the more vigorous and sensible exercises of the inclination and will of the soul"—things like hatred, desire, joy, delight, grief, hope, fear, gratitude, compassion, and zeal.

So when we speak of delight in God as the duty of man, we must realize it is not a simple thing. It is complex. One vigorous inclination in the human heart always must include others. Delight in the glory of God includes, for example, *hatred* for sin, *fear* of displeasing God, *hope* in the promises of God, *contentment* in the fellowship of God, *desire* for the final revelation of the Son of God, *exultation* in the redemption he accomplished, *grief* and *contrition* for failures of love, *gratitude* for undeserved benefits, *zeal* for the purposes of God, *hunger* for righteousness, and so on. Our duty toward God is that all our affections respond properly to his reality and so reflect his glory.

Edwards was utterly convinced that there is no true religion without holy affections. "He who has no religious affection is in a state of spiritual death and is wholly destitute of powerful quickening influences of the Spirit of God."[7]

But not only that; there is no true religion (or true saint) where there is no *perseverance* in holy affections. Perseverance is the mark of the elect and necessary to final salvation. "They that will not live godly lives find out for themselves that they are not elected; they that will live godly lives, have found out for themselves that they are elected."[8]

Edwards believed in justification by faith and thought much about how it related to perseverance. But the big issue then as now was, What is faith? Edwards said two crucial things. First, saving faith includes "belief of the truth, and an answerable disposition of the heart."[9] In other words, since faith is "an answerable disposition of the heart," it is not something different from the affections. Faith is "the soul's entirely embracing the revelation of Jesus Christ as our Savior." This embrace is an embrace of love: "Faith arises . . . from a principle of divine love" (cf. 1 Cor. 13:7; John 3:19;

5:42ff.). "Love to God is the main thing in saving faith." In other words, faith arises "from a spiritual taste and relish of what is excellent and divine."[10] Therefore, delight in God is the root of faith and faith is an essential expression of our delight in God. Contrary to much contemporary teaching, saving faith is by no means a mere decision of the will separate from the affections.

Second, saving faith is persevering faith. "For God has respect to perseverance [of faith] as being virtually in the first act [of saving faith]. And it is looked upon as if it were a property of that faith by which the sinner is then justified."[11] In other words, the first act of saving faith is like an acorn that has within it the spreading oak of all the subsequent perseverance in faith that the Bible says is necessary for final salvation. We are justified by faith once for all at our conversion, but we must (and most certainly will) also persevere in faith and its fruit in holy affections given to us in seed form at our conversion.

Therefore, Edwards says, "There is as much need of persons exercising care and diligence to persevere in order to their salvation, as there is of their attention and care to repent and be converted."[12] This will have tremendous implications for the way Edwards preaches. Preaching is a means of grace to assist the saints to persevere. Perseverance is necessary for final salvation. Therefore, every sermon is a "salvation sermon"—not just because of its aim to convert sinners, but also in its aim to preserve the holy affections of the saints and so enable them to confirm their calling and election and be saved.

In summary, then, when Jonathan Edwards becomes still and knows that God is God, the vision before his eyes is of an absolutely sovereign God, self-sufficient and all-sufficient, infinite in holiness, and therefore perfectly glorious. God's actions are never motivated to meet his deficiencies (since he has none), but are always motivated to display his sufficiency (which is infinite). He does what he does for the sake of his glory. Our duty and privilege, therefore, is to conform to this goal and reflect the value of God's glory by delighting in it. Our calling and our joy is to render visible God's glorious grace by trusting him with all our heart as long as we live.

Make God Supreme

The Preaching of Edwards

WHAT SORT OF PREACHING RESULTS from Edwards's vision of God? What sort of preaching did God use to ignite the Great Awakening in New England during Edwards's ministry at Northampton? Spiritual awakening is the sovereign work of God, to be sure. But he uses means, especially preaching. "Of his own will he brought us forth *by the word of truth*" (James 1:18). "It pleased God *through the folly of what we preach* to save those who believe" (1 Cor. 1:21).

I have tried to capture the essence of Edwards's preaching in ten characteristics. But I am so convinced of the value of these characteristics for our own day that I am going to call them ten characteristics of good preaching and present them as challenges to you, not just as facts about Edwards. I have gleaned these characteristics both from the way he preached and from his occasional comments about preaching.

1. Stir Up Holy Affections

Good preaching aims to stir up "holy affections"—things like hate for sin, delight in God, hope in his promises, gratitude for his mercy, desire for holiness, tender compassion. The reason for this is that the absence of holy affections in Christians is odious.

> The things of religion are so great, that there can be no suitableness in the exercises of our hearts, to their nature and importance, unless they be lively and powerful. In nothing is vigor in the actings of our inclinations so requisite, as in religion; and in nothing is lukewarmness so odious.[1]

Elsewhere Edwards remarked, "If true religion lies much in the *affections,* we may infer, that *such a way of preaching the word . . .* as has a tendency deeply to affect the hearts of those who attend . . . is much to be desired."[2]

Of course, the dignified clergy in Boston saw great danger in targeting the emotions like this. For example, Charles Chauncy charged that it was "a plain stubborn Fact, that the Passions have, generally, in these Times, been apply'd to, as though the main Thing in Religion was to throw them into Disturbance."[3] Edwards's answer was crafted and balanced.

> I don't think ministers are to be blamed for raising the affections of their hearers too high, if that which they are affected with be only that which is worthy of affection, and their affections are not raised beyond a proportion to their importance. . . . I should think myself in the way of my duty to raise the affections of my hearers as high as possibly I can, provided that they are affected with nothing but truth, and with affec-

tions that are not disagreeable to the nature of what they are affected with. I know it has long been fashionable to despise a very earnest and pathetical way of preaching; and they, and they only, have been valued as preachers, that have shown the greatest extent of learning, and strength of reason, and correctness of method and language: but I humbly conceive it has been for want of understanding, or duly considering human nature, that such preaching has been thought to have the greatest tendency to answer the ends of preaching; and the experience of the present and past ages abundantly confirms the same.[4]

Probably in our day someone would ask Edwards why he does not make external deeds of love and justice his goal rather than just the affections of the heart. The answer is that he does make behavior his aim, namely, by aiming to transform the spring of behavior—the affections. He chooses this strategy for two reasons. One is that a good tree can't bear bad fruit. The longest section of his great book *Religious Affections* is devoted to proving this thesis: "Gracious and holy affections have their exercise and fruit in Christian practice."[5] Edwards aims at the affections because they are the springs of all godly action. Make the tree good and its fruit will be good.

The other reason Edwards aims to stir up holy affections is that "no external fruit is good, which does not proceed from such exercises."[6] Outward acts of benevolence and piety that do not flow from the new and God-given affections of the heart, which delight to depend on God and seek his glory, are only legalism and have no value in honoring God. If you give your body to be burned and have not love, it profits nothing (1 Cor. 13:3).

Therefore, good preaching aims to stir up holy affections in those who hear. It targets the heart.

2. Enlighten the Mind

Yes, Edwards said, "Our people don't so much need to have their heads stored as to have their hearts touched and they stand in the greatest need of that sort of preaching that has the greatest tendency to do this."[7] But there is a world of difference between the way Edwards aims to move the hearts of his people and the way relational, psychologically oriented preachers today might try to move their hearers.

Edwards preached an ordination sermon in 1744 on the text about John the Baptist, "He was a burning and a shining light" (John 5:35 KJV). His main point was that a preacher must burn and shine. There must be heat in the heart and light in the mind— and no more heat than justified by the light.

> If a minister has light without heat, and entertains his auditory [hearers] with learned discourses, without a savour of the power of godliness, or any appearance of fervency of spirit, and zeal for God and the good of souls, he may gratify itching ears, and fill the heads of his people with empty notions; but it will not be very likely to reach their hearts, or save their souls. And if, on the other hand, he be driven on with a fierce and intemperate zeal, and vehement heat, without light, he will be likely to kindle the like unhallowed flame in his people, and to fire their corrupt passions and affections; but will make them never the better, nor lead them a step towards heaven, but drive them apace the other way.[8]

Heat *and* light. Burning *and* shining! It is crucial to bring light to the mind, because affections that do not rise from the mind's apprehension of truth are not holy affections. For example, he says:

> That faith, which is without spiritual light, is not the faith of the children of the light and of the day, but the presumption of the children of darkness. And therefore to press and urge them to believe, without any spiritual light or sight, tends greatly to help forward the delusions of the prince of darkness.[9]

He speaks even more strongly when he says:

> Suppose the religious affections of persons indeed arise from a strong persuasion of the truth of the Christian religion; their affections are not the better, unless it be a *reasonable* persuasion or conviction. By a reasonable conviction, I mean a conviction founded on *real evidence,* or upon that which is a good reason, or just ground of conviction.[10]

So the good preacher will make it his aim to give his hearers "good reason" and "just ground" for the affections he is trying to stir up. Edwards can never be brought forward as an example of one who manipulated emotions. He treated his hearers as creatures of reason and sought to move their hearts only by giving the light of truth to the mind.

Therefore, he taught that it is

> very profitable for ministers in their preaching, to endeavor clearly and distinctly to explain the doctrines of religion, and unravel the difficulties that attend them, and to confirm them with strength of reason and argumentation, and also to observe

some easy and clear method and order in their discourses, for the help of the understanding and memory.[11]

The reason for this is that good preaching aims to enlighten the mind of the hearers with divine truth. It was a wonderful combination that God used to awaken New England 250 years ago: heat and light, burning and shining, head and heart, deep doctrine and deep delight. May not God use this means again today as we seek to enlighten the mind and inflame the heart?

3. Saturate with Scripture

I say that good preaching is "saturated with Scripture" and not "based on Scripture" because Scripture is more (not less) than the basis for good preaching. Good preaching does not sit on Scripture like a basis and say other things. It oozes Scripture.

Again and again my advice to beginning preachers is, "Quote the text! Quote the text! Say the actual words of the text again and again. Show the people where your ideas are coming from." Most people do not easily see the connections a preacher sees between his words and the words of the text he is preaching from. They must be shown again and again by saturating the sermon with actual quotes from Scripture. Edwards expended great energy to write out whole passages in his sermon manuscripts that gave support for what he was saying. He quoted verse after verse that cast light on his theme. The reason Bible passages should saturate our sermons, according to Edwards, is that "they are as it were the beams of the light of the Sun of righteousness; they are the light by which ministers must be enlightened, and the light they are to hold forth to their hearers; and they are the fire whence their hearts and the hearts of their hearers must be enkindled."[12]

He looked back once on his early pastoral experience and said:

> I had then, and at other times, the greatest delight in the holy
> Scriptures, of any book whatsoever. Oftentimes in reading it,
> every word seemed to touch my heart. I felt a harmony between
> something in my heart, and those sweet and powerful words. I
> seemed often to see so much light exhibited by every sentence,
> and such a refreshing food communicated, that I could not get
> along in reading; often dwelling long on one sentence, to see
> the wonders contained in it; yet almost every sentence seemed
> to be full of wonders.[13]

One has to stand in awe of how thorough Edwards's knowledge
of the whole Bible was, especially in view of the fact that he was
also conversant with the best theological, moral, and philosophical
learning of his day. As a student he made this life resolution: "*Resolved*, To study the Scriptures so steadily, constantly, and frequently,
as that I may find, and plainly perceive, myself to grow in the
knowledge of the same."[14] "Steadily," "constantly," "frequently"—
this was the source of the wealth of Scripture in Edwards's sermons.

His practice in study was to take hundreds of notes on the Scriptures and pursue any thread of insight as far as he could.

> My method of study, from my first beginning the work of the
> ministry, has been very much by writing; applying myself, in this
> way, to improve every important hint; pursuing the clue to my
> utmost, when anything in reading, meditation, or conversation,
> has been suggested to my mind, that seemed to promise light in
> any weighty point; thus penning what appeared to me my best
> thoughts, on innumerable subjects, for my own benefit.[15]

His pen was his exegetical eye. Like Calvin (who said this in the introduction to the *Institutes*) he learned as he wrote and he wrote as he learned. In what he saw by this method he makes most of our hurried meditations on Scripture look very superficial.

The reason I love to read Edwards is the same reason I love to read the Puritans: It's like reading the Bible through the eyes of one who understands it deeply and feels it with all his heart. Good preaching (whatever name you put on it) is saturated with Scripture. And therefore, as Edwards says, the minister "must be well studied in divinity, well acquainted with the written word of God [and] mighty in the Scriptures."[16]

4. Employ Analogies and Images

Experience and Scripture teach that the heart is most powerfully touched not when the mind is entertaining abstract ideas, but when it is filled with vivid images of amazing reality. Edwards was, to be sure, a metaphysician and a philosopher of the highest order. He believed in the importance of theory. But he knew that abstractions kindled few affections. And new affections are the goal of preaching. So Edwards strained to make the glories of heaven look irresistibly beautiful and the torments of hell look intolerably horrible. And he sought to compare abstract theological truth to common events and experiences.

Sereno Dwight says that "those who are conversant with the writings of Edwards, need not be informed that all his works, even the most metaphysical, are rich in illustration, or that his sermons abound with imagery of every kind, adapted to make a powerful and lasting impression."[17]

In his most famous sermon, "Sinners in the Hands of an Angry God," Edwards referred to Revelation 19:15, which contains the phrase, "the winepress of the fierceness and wrath of Almighty God" (KJV). He says:

> The words are exceedingly terrible. If it had only been said, "the wrath of God," the words would have implied that which is infinitely dreadful: but it is "the fierceness and wrath of God." The fury of God! The fierceness of Jehovah! O how dreadful must that be! Who can utter or conceive what such expressions carry in them?[18]

There is Edwards's challenge to every preacher of the Word of God. Who can find images and analogies that come anywhere near creating the profound feelings we ought to have when we consider realities like hell and heaven? We dare not fault Edwards's images of hell unless we are prepared to fault the Bible. For in his own view (and I surely think he was right) he was only groping for language that might come close to what awesome realities are contained in biblical phrases like "the winepress of the fierceness and wrath of Almighty God."

Today we do just the opposite. We grope for circumlocutions of hell and create images as far from the horror of the biblical phrases as we can. Partly as a result, our attempts to make heaven look attractive and make grace look amazing often appear extremely pitiful. We would do well to labor with Edwards to find images and analogies that produce impressions in our people comparable to reality.

But it was not only heaven and hell that pushed Edwards to find analogies and images. He used the analogy of a surgeon with a scalpel to explain some kinds of preaching. He used the similarity of a human embryo to an animal embryo to show that at conversion a new life with all its new affections may be there but not yet show itself as fully distinct from the unregenerate. He pictured the pure heart with remaining impurities as a vat of fermenting liquor trying to get clean of all sediment. And he saw holiness in the soul as a garden of God with all manner of pleasant flowers. His sermons abound with images and analogies to give light to the understanding and heat to the affections.

5. Use Threat and Warning

Edwards did know his hell, but he knew his heaven even better. I can vividly recall the winter evenings in 1971–72 when my wife Noël and I sat on our couch in Munich, Germany, reading together Jonathan Edwards's sermon "Heaven Is a World of Love." What a magnificent vision! Surely if our people saw us preachers painting such pictures of glory and panting after God the way Edwards did, there would be a new awakening in the churches.

But those who have the largest hearts for heaven shudder most deeply at the horrors of hell. Edwards was fully persuaded that hell was real. "This doctrine is indeed awful and dreadful, yet 'tis of God."[19] Therefore, he esteemed the threats of Jesus as the strident tones of love. "Whoever says, 'You fool!' will be liable to the hell of fire" (Matt. 5:22). "It is better that you lose one of your members than that your whole body go into hell" (Matt. 5:30). "Fear him who can destroy both soul and body in hell" (Matt. 10:28). Edwards could not remain silent where Jesus was so vocal. Hell awaits every unconverted person. Love must warn them with the threats of the Lord.

The use of threat or warning in preaching to the saints is rare today for at least two reasons: First, it produces guilt and fear, which are considered to be unproductive. Second, it seems theologically inappropriate because the saints are secure and don't need to be warned or threatened. Edwards rejected both reasons. When fear and guilt correspond with the true state of things, it is reasonable and loving to stir them up. And, while the saints are secure in the omnipotent keeping power of God, their security proves itself in their willingness to give heed to biblical warnings and persevere in godliness. "Let anyone who thinks that he stands take heed lest he fall" (1 Cor. 10:12).

Edwards said that God set things up for the church in such a way "that when their *love* decays . . . *fear* should arise. They need *fear* then to restrain them from sin, [and] to excite them to care for the good of their souls. But God hath so ordered that when *love* rises . . . then fear should vanish, and be driven away."[20]

So on the one hand, Edwards says, "God's wrath and future punishment are proposed to all sorts of men, as motives to . . . obedience, not only to the wicked, but also to the godly."[21] And on the other hand, he says, "Holy love and hope are principles vastly more efficacious upon the heart, to make it tender, and to fill it with a dread of sin . . . than [is] a slavish fear of hell."[22] Preaching about hell is never an end in itself. You can't frighten anyone into heaven. Heaven is for people who love purity, not for people who simply loathe pain. Nevertheless, Edwards says, "Some talk of it as an unreasonable thing to think to fright persons to heaven; but I think it is a reasonable thing to endeavor to fright persons away from hell—'tis a reasonable thing to fright a person out of a house on fire."[23]

Therefore, good preaching will deliver the biblical messages of warning to congregations of saints just like Paul did when he said to the Galatians, "I warn you . . . that those who do such things will not inherit the kingdom of God" (Gal. 5:21). Or when he said, "Do not be arrogant, but fear" (Rom. 11:20, author's translation). Or when Peter said, "If you call on him as Father who judges impartially according to each one's deeds, conduct yourselves with fear throughout the time of your exile" (1 Pet. 1:17). Such warnings are the somber tones that help good preaching to display with lavish colors the magnificent promises and pictures of heaven like Paul did when he said to the Ephesians that in the coming ages God will "show the immeasurable riches of his grace in kindness toward us in Christ Jesus" (Eph. 2:7).

6. Plead for a Response

Can a Calvinist like Edwards really plead with people to flee hell and cherish heaven? Do not total depravity and unconditional election and irresistible grace make such pleading inconsistent?

Edwards learned his Calvinism from the Bible and therefore was spared many errors in his preaching. He did not infer that unconditional election or irresistible grace or supernatural regeneration or the inability of the natural man led to the conclusion that the use of pleading was inappropriate. He said, "Sinners . . . should be earnestly invited to come and accept of a Savior, and yield their hearts unto him, with all the winning, encouraging arguments for them . . . that the Gospel affords."[24]

I recall hearing a preacher in the Reformed tradition several years ago preach from 1 Corinthians 16, which ends with the fearful threat, "If anyone has no love for the Lord, let him be accursed" (v. 22). He alluded to it in passing, but there was no yearning or pleading with the people to love Christ and to escape the terrible curse. I marveled that this could be. There is a tradition of hyper-Calvinism that says that God's purpose to save the elect gives preachers warrant to invite to Christ only those who give evidence that they are already quickened and drawn by the Spirit. It breeds a kind of preaching that only informs but does not plead with sinners to repent. Edwards, like Spurgeon after him, knew that this was not authentic Calvinism; it was contrary to Scripture and unworthy of the Reformed tradition.

In fact, Edwards wrote a whole book, *The Freedom of the Will*, to show that

> God's moral government over mankind, His treating them as moral agents, making them the objects of His commands, counsels, calls, warnings, expostulations, promises, threatenings, rewards and punishments, is not inconsistent with a determining disposal of all events, of every kind, throughout the universe.[25]

In other words, pleading with our listeners to make a response to our preaching is not at odds with a high doctrine of the sovereignty of God.

When we preach, to be sure, it is *God* who effects the results for which we long. But that does not rule out earnest appeals for our people to respond. For as Edwards explains:

> We are not merely passive, nor yet does God do some, and we do the rest. But God does all, and we do all. God produces all, and we act all. For that is what he produces, viz. our own acts. God is the only proper author and fountain; we only are the proper actors. We are, in different respects, wholly passive and wholly active.
>
> In the Scriptures the same things are represented as from God and from us. God is said to convert [2 Tim. 2:25], and men are said to convert and turn [Acts 2:38]. God makes a new heart

[Ezek. 36:26], and we are commanded to make us a new heart [Ezek. 18:31]. God circumcises the heart [Deut. 30:6], and we are commanded to circumcise our own hearts [Deut. 10:16]. . . . These things are agreeable to that text, "God worketh in you both to will and to do [Phil. 2:13]."[26]

Therefore, Edwards pled with his people to respond to the Word of God and be saved. "Now, if you have any sort of prudence for your own salvation, and have not a mind to go to hell, improve this season! Now is the accepted time! Now is the day of salvation. . . . Do not harden your hearts at such a day as this!"[27] Almost every sermon has a long section called "Application" where Edwards screws in the implications of his doctrine and presses for a response. He did not give what is known today as an "altar call," but he did "call" and expostulate and plead for his people to respond to God.

So it seems that God has been pleased to give awakening power to preaching that does not shrink back from the loving threatenings of the Lord, and that lavishes the saints with incomparable promises of grace, and that pleads passionately and lovingly that no one hear the Word of God in vain. It is a tragedy to see pastors state the facts and sit down. Good preaching pleads with people to respond to the Word of God.

7. Probe the Workings of the Heart

Powerful preaching is like surgery. Under the anointing of the Holy Spirit, it locates, lances, and removes the infection of sin. Sereno Dwight, one of Edwards's early biographers, said of him, "His knowledge of the human heart, and its operations, has scarcely been equalled by that of any uninspired preacher."[28] My own experience as a patient on Edwards's operating table confirms this judgment.

How did Edwards get such a profound knowledge of the human soul? It was not from hobnobbing with the Northampton parishioners. Dwight said that he had never known of a man more constantly retired from the world to give himself to reading and contemplations. It may have begun with a typical Puritan bent toward introspection. On July 30, 1723, when he was nineteen years old, Edwards wrote in his diary, "Have concluded to endeavor to work myself into duties by searching and tracing back all the real reasons why I do them not, and narrowly searching out all the subtle subterfuges of my thoughts."[29] A week later he wrote, "Very much convinced of the extraordinary deceitfulness of the heart, and how exceedingly . . . appetite blinds the mind, and brings it into entire subjection."[30] So Dwight is certainly right when he says that much of Edwards's insight into the human heart came "from his thorough acquaintance with his own heart."[31]

A second thing that gave Edwards such a profound insight into the workings of the heart was the necessity of sorting out the wheat and the chaff in the intense religious experiences of his people during the Great Awakening. His book *Religious Affections*, which he had originally preached as sermons in 1742–43, is a devastating exposure of self-deception in religion. It probes relentlessly to the root of our depravity. This kind of sustained and careful examination of the religious experiences of his people gave Edwards a remarkable grasp of the works of their hearts.

A third cause of Edwards's knowledge of the human heart was his extraordinary insight into God's testimony about it in Scripture. For example, he notices in Galatians 4:15 that the religious experience of the Galatians had been so intense that they would have plucked out their eyes for Paul. But then Edwards notices also in verse 11 of that chapter that Paul says he might have "labored over you in vain." From this Edwards infers shrewdly that the height or intensity of religious affections (readiness to pluck out the eye) is no sure sign that they are genuine (since Paul's labor might have been in vain).[32] Years and years of this kind of study make for a profound surgeon of souls. It produces a preaching that uncovers the secret things of the heart. And more than once it has led to great awakening in the church.

Edwards said that every minister of the word "must be acquainted with experimental religion, and not ignorant of the inward operations of the Spirit of God, nor of Satan's devices."[33] Again and again when I read Edwards's sermons I have the profound experience of having myself laid bare. The secrets of my heart are plowed up. The deceitful workings of my heart are exposed. The potential beauty of new affections appears attractive. I find that they are even taking root as I read.

Edwards compared the preacher to a surgeon:

> To blame a minister for declaring the truth to those who are under awakenings, and not immediately administering comfort to them, is like blaming a surgeon because when he has begun to thrust in his lance, whereby he has already put his patient to great pain . . . he won't stay his hand, but goes on to thrust it in further, till he comes to the core of the wound. Such a compassionate physician, who as soon as his patient began to flinch, should withdraw his hand . . . would be one that would heal the hurt slightly, crying, "Peace, peace," when there is no peace.[34]

This analogy of the surgeon and the scalpel is indeed apt for his own preaching. We don't want to lie naked on the table, and we don't want to be cut, but oh, the joy of having the cancer out!

Therefore, good preaching, like good surgery, probes the workings of the human heart.

8. Yield to the Holy Spirit in Prayer

In 1735 Edwards preached a sermon entitled "The Most High, a Prayer-Hearing God." In it he said, "God has been pleased to constitute prayer to be antecedent to the bestowment of mercy; and he is pleased to bestow mercy in consequence of prayer, as though he were prevailed on by prayer."[35] The goal of preaching is utterly dependent on the mercy of God for its fulfillment. Therefore, the preacher must labor to put his preaching under divine influence by prayer.

By this means the Holy Spirit assists the preacher. But Edwards didn't believe the assistance came in the form of words being immediately suggested to the mind. If that's all the Spirit did, a preacher could be a devil and do his work. No, the Holy Spirit fills the heart with holy affections and the heart fills the mouth. "When a person is in an holy and lively frame in secret prayer, it will wonderfully supply him with matter and with expressions . . . [in] preaching."[36]

So Edwards counsels the young men of his day:

> Ministers, in order to be burning and shining lights, should walk closely with God, and keep near to Christ; that they may ever be enlightened and enkindled by him. And they should be much in seeking God, and conversing with him by prayer, who is the fountain of light and love.[37]

He tells us about his own experience with prayer early in his ministry, and I suspect that it became more precious rather than less. He says:

I spent most of my time in thinking of divine things, year after year; often walking alone in the woods, and solitary places, for meditation, soliloquy, and prayer, and converse with God; and it was always my manner, at such times, to sing forth my contemplations. I was almost constantly in ejaculatory prayer, wherever I was. Prayer seemed to be natural to me, as the breath by which the inward burnings of my heart had vent.[38]

Besides private prayer Edwards threw himself into the wider prayer movement of his day that was spreading from Scotland.

He wrote an entire book "to promote explicit agreement and visible union of God's people in extraordinary prayer for the revival of religion and advancement of Christ's kingdom."[39] The secret prayer of the preacher and the concerts of prayer among the people conspire in the mercy of God to bring down the demonstration of the Spirit and of power.

Good preaching is born of good praying. And it will come forth with the power that caused the Great Awakening when it is delivered under the mighty prayer-wrought influence of the Holy Spirit.

9. Be Broken and Tenderhearted

Good preaching comes from a spirit of brokenness and tenderness. For all his authority and power Jesus was attractive because he was "gentle and lowly in heart," which made him a place of rest (Matt. 11:29). "When he saw the crowds, he had compassion for them, because they were harassed and helpless, like sheep without a shepherd" (Matt. 9:36). There is in the Spirit-filled preacher a tender affection that sweetens every promise and softens with tears every warning and rebuke. "We were gentle among you, like a nursing mother taking care of her own children. So, being affectionately desirous of you, we were ready to share with you not only the gospel of God but also our own selves, because you had become very dear to us" (1 Thess. 2:7–8).

One of the secrets of Edwards's power in the pulpit was the "brokenhearted" tenderness with which he could address the weightiest matters. In his own words we catch the scent of this demeanor:

All gracious affections . . . are brokenhearted affections. A truly Christian love . . . is a humble brokenhearted love. The desires of the saints, however earnest, are humble desires; their hope is an humble hope; and their joy, even when it is unspeakable, and full of glory, is a humble, brokenhearted joy, and leaves the Christian more poor in spirit, and more like a little child and more disposed to an universal lowliness of behavior.[40]

Genuine spiritual power in the pulpit is not synonymous with loudness. Hard hearts are not likely to be broken by shrill voices. Edwards was persuaded from Scripture that "gracious affections do not tend to make men bold, forward, noisy, and boisterous; but rather to speak trembling."[41] The eye of divine blessing is upon the meek and trembling: "This is the one to whom I will look [says the Lord]: he who is humble and contrite in spirit and trembles at my word" (Isa. 66:2).

Therefore, Edwards says:

Ministers should be persons of the same quiet, lamb-like spirit that Christ was of . . . the same spirit of forgiveness of injuries; the same spirit of charity, of fervent love and extensive benevolence; the same disposition to pity the miserable, to weep with those that weep, to help men under their calamities of both soul and body, to hear and grant the requests of the needy, and relieve the afflicted; the same spirit of condescension to the poor and mean, tenderness and gentleness towards the weak, and great and effectual love to enemies.[42]

The spirit we long to see in our people must be in ourselves first. But that will never happen until, as Edwards says, we know our own emptiness and helplessness and terrible sinfulness. Edwards lived in a kind of spiraling oscillation between humiliation for his sin and exultation in his Savior. He describes his experience like this:

Often since I lived in this town, I have had very affecting views of my own sinfulness and vileness; very frequently to such a degree as to hold me in a kind of loud weeping, sometimes for a considerable time together; so that I have often been forced to shut myself up.[43]

It is not hard to imagine the depth of earnestness that this kind of experience brought to the preaching of God's Word.

But of course one is on the precipice of despair when one focuses only on sin. This was not Edwards's aim nor his experience. For him there was a response to guilt that made it an intensely evangelical and liberating experience:

I love to think of coming to Christ, to receive salvation of him, poor in spirit, and quite empty of self, humbly exalting him alone; cut off entirely from my own root, in order to grow into, and out of Christ; to have God in Christ be my all in all.[44]

This is the supremacy of God in the life of the preacher that leads straight to God's supremacy in preaching.

When we speak of Edwards's intensity, it is plain that it was not a harsh and loud and belligerent thing. Edwards's power was not in rhetorical flourish or ear-splitting thunders. It was born in brokenhearted affections.

Edwards was described by Thomas Prince as "a preacher of a low and moderate voice, a natural way of delivery; and without any agitation of body, or anything else in the manner to excite attention; except his habitual and great solemnity, looking and speaking as in the presence of God."[45] Edwards stands as a rare testimony to the truth that good preaching—preaching that makes God supreme—comes from a spirit of brokenness and tenderness.

10. Be Intense

Good preaching gives the impression that something very great is at stake. With Edwards's view of the reality of heaven and hell and the necessity of persevering in a life of holy affections and godliness, eternity was at stake every Sunday. This sets him off from the average preacher today. Our emotional rejection of hell and our facile view of conversion and the abundant false security we purvey have created an atmosphere in which the great biblical intensity of preaching is almost impossible.

Edwards so believed in the realities of which he spoke, and so longed for their reality to stagger his people, that when George Whitefield preached these realities with power in Edwards's pulpit, Edwards wept during the whole service. Edwards could no more imagine speaking in a cold or casual or indifferent or flippant manner about the great things of God than he could imagine a father discussing coolly the collapse of a flaming house upon his children.[46]

Lack of intensity in preaching can only communicate that the preacher does not believe or has never been seriously gripped by the reality of which he speaks—or that the subject matter is insignificant. This was never the case with Edwards. He stood in continual awe at the weight of the truth he was charged to proclaim.

One contemporary said that Edwards's eloquence was

> the power of presenting an important truth before an audience, with overwhelming weight of argument, and with such intenseness of feeling, that the whole soul of the speaker is thrown into every part of the conception and delivery; so that the solemn attention of the whole audience is riveted, from the beginning to the close, and impressions are left that cannot be effaced.[47]

In his introduction to John Gillies's *Historical Collections of Accounts of Revival,* Horatius Bonar in 1845 described the kind of preachers God had been pleased to use to awaken his church through the centuries:

> They felt their infinite responsibility as stewards of the mysteries of God and shepherds appointed by the Chief Shepherd to gather in and watch over souls. They lived and labored and preached like men on whose lips the immortality of thousands hung. Everything they did and spoke bore the stamp of earnestness, and proclaimed to all with whom they came into contact that the matters about which they had been sent to treat were of infinite moment. . . . Their preaching seems to have been of the most masculine and fearless kind, falling on the audience with tremendous power. It was not vehement, it was not fierce, it was not noisy; it was far too solemn to be such; it was massive, weighty, cutting, piercing, sharper than a two-edged sword.[48]

So it was with Jonathan Edwards just 250 years ago. By precept and example Edwards calls us to "an exceeding affectionate way of preaching about the great things of religion" and to flee from a "moderate, dull indifferent way of speaking."[49] We simply must signify, without melodrama or affectation, that the reality behind our message is breathtaking.

Of course, that assumes that we have seen the God of Jonathan Edwards. If we don't share the greatness of his vision of God, we will not approach the greatness of his preaching. On the other hand, if God in his grace should see fit to open our eyes to the vision of Edwards, if we were granted to taste the sweet sovereignty of the Almighty the way Edwards tasted it, then a renewal of the pulpit in our day would be possible— indeed inevitable.

PART 3

AFTER THIRTY-THREE YEARS

God Still Supreme in Preaching and Ministry

8

Jonathan Edwards
Thirty-Three Years Later

Clarifications and Confirmation

AFTER MY THIRTY-THREE YEARS of pastoral ministry, Jonathan Edwards is still inspiring and teaching me. When I entered the pastoral ministry in 1980, six volumes of the Yale University *Works of Jonathan Edwards* had been published. Today all twenty-five volumes are complete. Even more remarkable, personal computers and the internet were invented! I began to use a computer in 1985. Today virtually everything still in existence that Jonathan Edwards ever wrote is available online to read for free through the Jonathan Edwards Center at Yale University (http://edwards.yale .edu/archive/), seventy-three volumes total.

Hero, Friend, Guide

I was thirty-four years old when I became a pastor. Jonathan Edwards was a hero, a friend—as much as you can have friends who are deceased—and the most influential dead theologian in my life, outside the writers of the Bible. His *Dissertation Concerning the End for Which God Created the World* had shaped all my thinking about why I, and the church, and the world, existed. His insight that "God is glorified not only by His glory's being *seen*, but by its being *rejoiced in*"[1] was a cornerstone in the foundation of my whole view of preaching and ministry. And his *Freedom of the Will* had long ago settled the massive question of whether God really governs all things.

I cannot overstate the importance of a preacher having clear and magnificent views of these things: the end for which God created the world, the way human joy fits into that, and the sovereignty of God's grace in the way he saves sinners and rules the world. Solid biblical views on these things give strength to our preaching and to our people. They are like ballast in the boat of our lives. They keep us upright in the winds of false doctrine and in the storms of calamity.

Now my thirty-three years as a pastor are past. And at age sixty-eight, I testify that Jonathan Edwards is still a great guide and inspiration to me. I draw attention to this because pastors who last a long time, especially in one place, need spiritually superior helpers. We all tend to get weary. We tend to coast and to start seeing well-worn sights and saying well-worn words. We must be ignited afresh, over and over. How does the Holy Spirit do this? One way he does it is by preserving for us in writing the glorious things great lovers of God have seen.

Stunned Awake by "Christ's Agony"

Edwards is that source of ignition for me. For example, about three years ago I was depleted and badly in need of fresh fire in my soul for Christ. I desperately did not want the words of Paul, "For the sake of Christ I count everything as loss," to be empty sounds in my mouth. I wanted to know him better than I know anyone, and love him more than I loved anyone.

So I opened my iPad and found the collected works of Edwards and chose at random to read a sermon called "Christ's Agony."[2] To this day I can remember where I was sitting in my living room, what corner of the couch, as I read this message. It was stunning. I could not stop till I was done. So penetrating. So full of wine from the crushing and wringing of these grape-texts. So many questions posed. Such answers!

This has happened countless times for me. Pastors need a pastor. And we need a seer. A visionary. A worshiper. A poet—not one that rhymes, necessarily, but one who can say with clarity and compelling power what they have seen. I have never read anyone who sees like Edwards. And for me, his words impart wonder and worship.

So that much has remained the same through the years since I first wrote this book: Edwards is still a great model and mentor and mover for the hungry preacher. I had only been preaching a few years when I wrote my first chapters on Edwards. Now, after three decades of preaching, I say Amen to what I wrote. If I were starting over, I would still start like that.

Clarifications and a Confirmation

Edwards has not only remained one of my primary inspirations but he has also brought increasing clarity and focus to some things that were less clear to me in the early days— things that are essential for good preaching. Here, I will use one of Edwards's sermons that I first encountered in the final (twenty-fifth) volume of the Yale

Works published in 2006. From it, I will illustrate three clarifications for my own thinking and one confirmation.

In December 1744, Jonathan Edwards preached a sermon foreshadowing his book *The End for Which God Created the World*, which he completed eleven years later, three years before he died. The sermon's title is "Approaching the End of God's Grand Design."[3]

It is the kind of sermon that draws me back again and again to Edwards, to rescue me from the spiritual stranglehold of small things. It's this kind of seeing that creates a seedbed of Big-God Theology and Big-God Preaching.

The biblical text for the sermon is Revelation 21:6: "And he said to me, 'It is done!'" Edwards states the "Doctrine"—the Puritans' term for the thesis, or the main point—"There is a time coming when God's grand design in all his various works and dispensations from age to age will be completed and his end fully obtained." In other words, a time when God will say, "It is done."

Then Edwards asks: "What is this one great design that God has in view in all his works and dispensations?" He answers:

> 'Tis to present to his Son a spouse in perfect glory from amongst sinful, miserable mankind, blessing all that comply with his will in this matter and destroying all his enemies that oppose it, and so to communicate and glorify himself through Jesus Christ, God-man.[4]

That is a very carefully crafted sentence. It points to three emphases that have become clearer and more central to my preaching over the years.

A Clearer Sight of the Centrality of Christ

The first emphasis is the supremacy of Christ, the centrality of Christ, in the final end of God's purpose in creation and history. The longer I have preached, the more prominent the Christological dimension of God's purposes has become. Is it not remarkable that Edwards defines the "great design that God has in view in all his works and dispensations" as "to present to his Son a spouse" and "so to communicate himself through Jesus Christ, God-man"?

Or as he says later, "The one grand medium by which God glorifies himself in all is Jesus Christ, God-man."[5] It is not easy for a preacher to discern week in and week out whether his emphases are properly theocentric or Christocentric. Part of the problem here is with our spatial metaphors: *-centric*. There are times when God the Father, or God *per se*, is "central" to a text and to our perception of reality. And there are times when God the Son is "central" to a text and to our perception of reality.

Changing the metaphor from "center" to "end" or "ultimate goal," what Edwards clarifies is that this emphasis on the centrality of Christ in God's "grand design" is preserved not by making Christ the ultimate "end" but rather the ever-present, essential, indispensable, divine agent *through whom* God communicates himself and glorifies himself as the ultimate end.

This is clearly biblical.

God exalted Jesus Christ with a name above every name, so that "every tongue [will] confess that Jesus Christ is Lord, *to the glory of God the Father*" (Phil. 2:11). The glory of the Father is the ultimate end *through* the exaltation of Jesus. "We also rejoice in God *through our Lord Jesus Christ, through whom* we have now received reconciliation" (Rom. 5:11).

Whoever serves, [let him serve] as one who serves by the strength that God supplies—in order that in everything God may be glorified *through Jesus Christ.* To him belong glory and dominion forever and ever. Amen. (1 Pet. 4:11)

But what became clearer to me as my ministry matured is the utter indispensability of highlighting Jesus Christ, the God-man, as essential to the way God makes himself the grand design of creation.

These days I hear Paul's words with greater weight than ever: "We preach Christ" (1 Cor. 1:23). "Him we proclaim" (Col. 1:28). "What we proclaim is not ourselves, but Jesus Christ as Lord" (2 Cor. 4:5). "To me . . . this grace was given, to preach to the Gentiles the unsearchable riches of Christ" (Eph. 3:8).

I don't hear this summons to preach Christ only in relation to one work of Christ, but in relation to the great end of all creation and history and redemption and consummation. It all really is "centered" on Jesus as the Great Actor of God's design. All things—absolutely all things—"were created *through* him and *for* him" (Col. 1:16). This role in creation and all of history and eternity must be lifted up again and again in preaching. As plain as it is in the Bible, Edwards helped clarify that for me.

A Clearer Sense of God's Self-Communication

The second clarification is that God's great end—grand design—in creation is not only to glorify himself but to communicate himself. This has always been implicit in my understanding of how God is glorified by our being satisfied in him, but it has become clearer to me that God's self-glorification is properly emphasized when we keep it connected to his self-communication.

God's end in the creation of the world consists in these two things, viz. to communicate himself and to glorify himself. God created the world to communicate himself, not to receive anything.[6]

These two things ought [not] to be separated when we speak of God's end in the creation of the world. . . . Indeed, God's communicating himself and glorifying [himself] ought not to be looked upon as though they were two distinct ends, but as what together makes one last end, as glorifying God and enjoying [God] make one chief end of man. For God glorifies himself in communicating himself, and he communicates himself in glorifying himself.[7]

The reason this clarification matters is that it protects God's self-glorification from being disconnected with his self-giving. Almost no one finds fault with saying, "God gives himself to us." Few people find fault with saying, "God gives himself to us for our enjoyment." But many people find fault with saying, "God glorifies himself." Nevertheless, it is clear from the whole scope of Scripture that he does.[8]

Therefore, to help people embrace the whole truth, it is wise to keep these two truths together, especially since, as Edwards says, they are "one last end." In all his self-glorifying acts in the world, God is revealing and giving himself to all who will receive him as their portion and their treasure. His self-glorifying is not only a "show," but a gift of himself.

A Clearer Comprehension of the Prominence of Union with Christ

The third clarification is the importance of the doctrine of union between Christ and his bride, his church. Edwards is striking in the way he relates the church to the ultimate end of God in creation.

The principal means by which God glorifies his Son in the world . . . is by providing him a spouse, to be presented [to] him in perfect union, in perfect purity, beauty and glory.

[Since God's aim was to display the goodness of Christ, he chose a bride for him who was] fit not to give but receive good, one . . . that was remarkably empty and poor in herself . . . fallen, miserable, helpless: a state wherein [her] emptiness and need of goodness did more remarkably appear.[9]

And because the design was that Christ should communicate goodness, therefore such an one was chosen that needed that Christ should suffer, and it was the will of Christ to suffer because suffering is the greatest expression of goodness and manifestation of kindness.

The great design was that Christ in this way should procure or obtain this his spouse, bring her to come to him, present her to himself and make her perfectly beautiful, perfectly and unspeakably happy. . . . And this is the way that God the Father intended to glorify his Son.[10]

This "perfect union"[11] between Christ and his church, "in perfect purity, beauty and glory," is an astonishing way of seeing the ultimate end of all creation. The self-giving of God reaches its exquisite apex in the self-giving of the Son to his bride in bringing her to share his holiness and know a fellowship and union beyond all human comprehension (Eph. 3:19, "the love of Christ that surpasses knowledge").

I have come to see more clearly, as time has gone by, that imbedded in my understanding of God's great self-glorifying, self-communicating goal in history, our union with Christ is essential.

As it is pervasive in the New Testament,[12] so it should be an ever-present backdrop or foundation for all that we preach. Edwards has helped me see this and I am thankful.

A Sweet Confirmation of Christian Hedonism

Finally, this sermon, "Approaching the End of God's Grand Design," has been a sweet confirmation of a forty-five-year emphasis of mine, namely, that *God is most glorified in us when we are most satisfied in him*. Perhaps you passed over it quickly in a prior quote. So here it is again:

> Indeed, God's communicating himself and glorifying [himself] ought not to be looked upon as though they were two distinct ends, but as what together makes one last end, *as glorifying God and enjoying [God] make one chief end* of man.[13]

"Glorifying and enjoying God make one chief end." When the Westminster divines said, "The chief end of man is to glorify God and enjoy him forever," they used the singular "end," not the plural "ends." I have devoted most of my life to defending and explaining and applying this reality: God is glorified *by* our enjoying him. I would not change that.

I believe with all my heart that this truth is crucial to preaching and that preaching is uniquely suited for this truth (see the preface to the second edition). Therefore, I rejoice in the help that Edwards has been not only in seeing this truth for the first time forty-five years ago, but in his confirming and deepening it over the years. I believe this truth lies at the heart of biblically faithful, God-exalting, soul-saving, and soul-satisfying preaching.

Perhaps I may be indulged a closing prayer of thanks:

What a gift. Thank you, Lord Jesus, for opening the eyes of Jonathan Edwards. Thank you for expanding his heart to sense your greatness where most of us pass by unmoved. Thank you for preserving so much of his seeing and savoring for us. And thank you for leading me again and again back to this soul-expanding spring of life. Amen.

9

In Honor of Tethered Preaching

John Calvin and the Entertaining Pastor

AFTER THIRTY-THREE YEARS of pastoral ministry and constant preaching, I love, revere, and hunger for the Bible more than I ever have. At age sixty-eight, my driving desire is to see more clearly what the Bible teaches, savor more deeply the God it reveals, and speak more compellingly its whole counsel to as many people as I can.

I feel that I have barely scratched the surface. Every day I see in the Bible evidences of how much more truth there is to see and how much more of God there is to know. I am glad I have given my life to this. I desire the same for thousands of young preachers.

I write this chapter out of concern that many younger preachers are attracted more to being a culturally savvy entertainer than a biblically tethered preacher. I write in honor of tethered preaching. The church and the world need this a thousand times more than they need to be entertained in the pulpit (or strolling around on stage). Why is that?

It Is a Safe and Satisfying Tether

The Bible tethers us to reality. We are not free to think and speak whatever might enter our minds or whatever might be pleasing to any given audience—except God. I hope I speak for you when I say, by personal calling and Scripture, I am bound to the Word of God and to the preaching of what the Bible says.

There are few things that burden me more, or refresh me more, than saying what I see in the Bible. I love to see what God says in the Bible. I love to savor it. And I love to say it. I believe with all my heart that this is the way God has appointed for all his preachers not to waste our lives.

God's Word is true. The Bible is the only completely true book in the world. It is inspired by God. Rightly understood and followed, it will lead us to everlasting joy with him. There is no greater book or greater truth.

Calvin's Vastness in Being Fettered to the Scriptures

The implications of this for preaching are immense. Jonathan Edwards is not my only hero nor the only one who has inspired me to give my life to seeing and savoring what the Bible reveals. John Calvin's commitment to preach the vast terrain of the Bible is stunningly inspiring.

With the other Reformers, Calvin rescued the Scriptures from their subordination to tradition in the medieval church. The Reformation, let us thank God, was the recovery of the unique and supreme authority of Scripture over church authority. Commenting on John 17:20, Calvin wrote,

> Woe to the Papists, whose faith is so far removed from this rule, that they are not ashamed to vomit out this horrid blasphemy,

that there is nothing in Scripture but what is ambiguous, and may be turned in a variety of ways. The tradition of the Church is therefore their only authoritative guide to what they shall believe. But let us remember that the Son of God, who alone is competent to judge, does not approve of any other faith than that which is drawn from the doctrine of the apostles, and sure information of that doctrine will be found no where else than in their writings.[1]

Calvin's preaching inspires me to press on with this great and glorious task of heralding the Word of God. I feel the force of what he says when, in a letter to Cardinal Sadoleto, he prays,

Lord, you have enlightened me with the brightness of your Spirit. You have put your Word as a lamp to my feet. The clouds which before now veiled your glory have been dispelled by it, and the blessings of your Anointed have shone clearly upon my eyes. What I have learnt from your mouth (that is to say, from your Word) I will distribute faithfully to your church.[2]

For Calvin, preaching was tethered to the Bible. "What I have learnt from your mouth I will distribute faithfully to your church." That is why he preached through books of the Bible so relentlessly.[3] Oh, that today young preachers were as moved by Calvin's example as by the audience-holding powers of the entertaining talks.

In honor of tethered preaching, let me try to explain what I mean by entertainment in the pulpit and what the differences are between preaching that is tethered to the Word of God and preaching that ranges free and leans toward entertainment.

What Is an Entertainment-Oriented Preacher?

The difference between an entertainment-oriented preacher and a Bible-oriented preacher is the presence or absence of a *manifest connection* between the preacher's words and the Bible as the authorization of what he says.

The entertainment-oriented preacher gives the impression that he is not tethered to an authoritative book in what he says. What he says doesn't seem to be shaped and constrained by an authority outside himself. He gives the impression that what he says has significance for reasons other than the fact that it manifestly expresses the meaning and significance of the Bible. So he seems untethered to objective authority.

The entertainment-oriented preacher seems to be at ease talking about many things that are not drawn out of the Bible. In his message, he seems to enjoy talking about other things more than what the Bible teaches. His words seem to have a self-standing worth as interesting or fun. They are entertaining. But they don't give the impression that this man stands as the representative of God before God's people to deliver God's message.

What Is a Bible-Oriented Preacher?

On the other hand, the Bible-oriented preacher does see himself that way— "I am God's representative sent to God's people to deliver a message from God." He feels the weight and the joy of this trust. He knows that the only way a man can dare to assume such a position is with a trembling sense of unworthy servanthood under the authority of the Bible. He knows that the only way he can deliver God's message to God's people is by rooting it in, and saturating it with, God's own revelation in the Bible.

The Bible-oriented preacher wants the congregation to know that *his* words, if they have any abiding worth, are in accord with *God's* words. He wants this to be obvious to them. That is the root of his humility and his authority. Therefore, he constantly tries to show the people that his ideas are coming from the Bible.

He is hesitant to go too far toward points that are not demonstrable from the Bible. He may illustrate and he may narrate a story, but he makes a beeline back to the Bible. He knows stories and anecdotes are entertaining. People like them. But he knows even more that his lasting authority and impact is not in the extrabiblical illustration, but in the manifestly biblical truth.

His stories and illustrations are constrained and reined in by his hesitancy to lead the consciousness of his hearers away from the sense that this message is based on and expressive of what the Bible says. A sense of submission to the Bible, and a sense that the Bible alone has words of true and lasting significance for our people, mark the Bible-oriented preacher but not the entertainment-oriented preacher.

People leave the preaching of the Bible-oriented preacher with a sense that the Bible is supremely authoritative and important and wonderfully good news. They feel less entertained than struck by the greatness of God and the weighty power of his Word.

What People Really Need from You

Therefore, I plead with you, do not put your faith in the way people are pleased with entertaining preaching, but put your faith in the way they are helped by the power of God's Word explained and driven home with blood-earnest, not breezy, application.

One of the main points of this book is that people are starving for the grandeur of God. Most of them don't know that this is what their hearts are longing for. It is the great work of the preacher to show them the greatness of God, Christ, salvation, life, death, heaven, hell, and the ways of God in the world. It is our job to help them see that their addiction to entertainment is like addiction to sugar. It gives ever-shorter highs and then lets you fall lower and lower. But a steady diet of Bible-saturated truth and wonder enlarges the soul and strengthens the heart, and makes Jesus precious beyond words.

This happens when the preacher is persuaded that everything he says must be tethered to the Bible, and when he helps his people see that tethering and base their lives on it. So I hope you join me in praying,

Lord, tether us to your mighty Word. Cause me and all preachers to show the people that our word is powerless and insignificant in comparison with yours. Grant us to stand before our people as messengers sent with God's message to God's people in God's name by God's Spirit. May we tremble at this responsibility. Protect us from trifling with this holy moment before your people. Amen.

10

Preaching as Concept Creation, Not Just Contextualization

IN THE LAST DECADE OF my thirty-three-year pastorate, this idea of preaching as concept creation crystalized for me. It grew out of the missiological struggle of contextualization—both among subcultures I was familiar with (for example, church planting that focuses on twentysomethings), as well as people groups that are culturally very different. It struck me that most of the attention seemed to be on the challenges of contextualization and little was on the opposite challenge of creating concepts and categories in people that they do not bring to the gospel.

Not without the Holy Spirit
It became clear to me, as never before, that as we think seriously about contextualizing the message of the Bible we must also labor to bring about, in the minds of our listeners, conceptual categories that may be missing from their mental framework. It may be that if we only use the thought structures our audience already has, some

crucial biblical truths may remain unintelligible, no matter how much contextualizing we do.

This work of concept creation is harder than contextualization, but just as important. We must pray and preach so that a new mental framework is created for seeing the world. Ultimately, this is not our doing. God must do it. The categories that make the biblical message look foolish are deeply rooted in sinful human nature. "The natural person does not accept the things of the Spirit of God, for they are folly to him, and he is not able to understand them because they are spiritually discerned" (1 Cor. 2:14).

Not without the Means of Thinking and Preaching

Part of what the Spirit does in overcoming human resistance is to humble us to the point where we can let go of ingrained patterns of thought. But the Spirit does this through preaching and teaching. "Since, in the wisdom of God, the world did not know God through wisdom [that is, through its cherished ways of thinking], it pleased God through the folly of what we preach to save those who believe" (1:21).

God brings about this new seeing and understanding and believing. But he uses us to do it. So we should give as much effort to helping people have new, biblical categories of thought as we do to contextualizing the gospel to the categories they already have. Both are crucial.

Examples of Category Creation

Here are a few examples of biblical truths that most fallen minds have little or no conceptual categories for conceiving. What we need in our day—as always—are witnesses who don't distort the truth by overzealous contextualizing but rather awaken a place for it in minds that have new Spirit-created categories.

I realize there are very controversial statements in the following list. This is largely why new categories of thinking are required to grasp them. My aim here is not to persuade you of any one of these statements, but to simply illustrate the kind of challenge we face in preaching: it is not just contextualization, but also concept creation.

1. All persons are accountable for their choices, and all their choices are infallibly and decisively ordained by God.

   He works all things according to the counsel of his will (Eph. 1:11).

   On the day of judgment people will give account for every careless word they speak (Matt. 12:36).

2. It is not sin in God to will that there be sin.

   As for you, you meant evil against me, but God meant it [the evil acts of Joseph's brothers] for good (Gen. 50:20).

3. The acts that God decrees will come to pass are not always the same as what he commands that we do, and may indeed be the opposite.

   For example, he may command, "Thou shalt not kill," and decree that his Son be killed: "It was the will of the Lord to crush him" (Isa. 53:10; see Acts 4:27–28).

4. God's ultimate goal is the exaltation and display of his own glory, and this self-exalting aim is at the heart of what it means for him to love us.

And now, Father, glorify me in your own presence with the glory that I had with you before the world existed (John 17:5).

Father, I desire that they also, whom you have given me, may be with me where I am, to see my glory (17:24).

5. Sin is not primarily what hurts man but what belittles God by expressing unbelief or indifference to his superior worth.

My people have committed two evils: they have forsaken me, the fountain of living waters, and hewed out cisterns for themselves, broken cisterns that can hold no water (Jer. 2:13).

Against you, you only, have I sinned and done what is evil in your sight (Ps. 51:4).

6. God is perfectly just and orders the complete destruction of the inhabitants of Canaan.

Shall not the Judge of all the earth do what is just? (Gen. 18:25).

But in the cities of these peoples that the Lord your God is giving you for an inheritance, you shall save alive nothing that breathes (Deut. 20:16).

7. The key to the Christian life is learning the secret of acting in such a way that our acts are done as the acts of Another.

   If we live by the Spirit, let us also keep in step with the Spirit (Gal. 5:25).

   If by the Spirit you put to death the deeds of the body, you will live (Rom. 8:13).

8. Those who belong to Christ have crucified the flesh, and they must daily kill it.

   And those who belong to Christ Jesus have crucified the flesh with its passions and desires (Gal. 5:24).

   Put to death therefore what is earthly in you (Col. 3:5).

9. "The virgin shall conceive and bear a son" (Matt. 1:23).

10. Jesus said to them, "Truly, truly, I say to you, before Abraham was, I am" (John 8:58).

Not Either-Or but Both-And

The point is this: our job is much harder than only contextualizing biblical categories into the categories of other people. That is hard enough. But the fact is there are some biblical categories and concepts that will not fit into the categories of other people no matter how gifted at contextualization we are. These categories and concepts must be created. This is finally the work of the Holy Spirit, but he uses human means. And we must give our best to this as well as to contextualization.

Father of mercies, we realize we are utterly dependent on you for this great and impossible work of preaching. We know that the people who need us most are least able to understand what we say. They are dead in trespasses and sins. The cross is a stumbling block and foolishness to them. Yet we long to be used to save them and transform their minds and impart to them "the mind of Christ." We believe you have appointed preaching for this great task. We embrace this impossibility and ask you to do through us far more than we could ever ask or think. In Jesus's name, Amen.

11

Thirty Reasons Why It Is a Great Thing to Be a Pastor

AFTER THIRTY-THREE YEARS in the pastoral ministry, I prepared these thirty reasons why it is a great thing to be a pastor in preparation for meeting with a group of young church planters. There are more reasons than these thirty, but these are basic and crucial.

I stand amazed and full of thankfulness that I had this privilege for so long. How good God has been to me. There is no chapter of my life I would exchange. I only wish I had lived each more humbly, more fully, and more fruitfully. God was faithful. The people were ever-gracious, and their love covered a multitude of sins. This pastoral chapter was the longest. When I stepped down as pastor, half my life had been spent pastoring Bethlehem Baptist Church in Minneapolis, Minnesota.

This chapter may be viewed as my song of praise that God would entrust such a calling to mere men—mere, sinful, fallible, finite men. My prayer, which I will pray at the end, is that this song of amazed privilege will inspire many to give themselves to this great work.

1. God is the greatest Reality in the universe. And pastors swim in that sea with ever-replenished joy.

   I am the Lord, and there is no other, besides me there is no God (Isa. 45:5).

   Oh, the depth of the riches and wisdom and knowledge of God! How unsearchable are his judgments and how inscrutable his ways! "For who has known the mind of the Lord, or who has been his counselor?" "Or who has given a gift to him that he might be repaid?" For from him and through him and to him are all things. To him be glory forever. Amen (Rom. 11:33–36).

2. Jesus is the greatest Savior, Master, and Friend that ever was or ever will be. And pastors contemplate and commend him every day.

   Greater love has no one than this, that someone lay down his life for his friends (John 15:13).

   At the name of Jesus every knee should bow, in heaven and on earth and under the earth, and every tongue confess that Jesus Christ is Lord, to the glory of God the Father (Phil. 2:10–11).

   No longer do I call you servants, for the servant does not know what his master is doing; but I have called you friends, for all that I have heard from my Father I have made known to you (John 15:15).

Remember Jesus Christ, risen from the dead, the offspring of David, as preached in my gospel (2 Tim. 2:8).

3. The Holy Spirit is the greatest Helper in the world. And pastors are driven to have his fullness constantly.

I will ask the Father, and he will give you another Helper, to be with you forever. . . . It is to your advantage that I go away, for if I do not go away, the Helper will not come to you. But if I go, I will send him to you (John 14:16; 16:7).

Does he who supplies the Spirit to you and works miracles among you do so by works of the law, or by hearing with faith? (Gal. 3:5).

Do not get drunk with wine, for that is debauchery, but be filled with the Spirit (Eph. 5:18).

4. The Bible is the greatest book there is. And pastors delight to meditate on it day and night.

The words of the Lord are pure words, like silver refined in a furnace on the ground, purified seven times (Ps. 12:6).

Blessed is the man who walks not in the counsel of the wicked, nor stands in the way of sinners, nor sits in the seat of scoffers; but his delight is in the law of the Lord and on his law he meditates day and night (1:1–2).

The rules of the Lord are true, and righteous altogether. More to be desired are they than gold, even much fine gold; sweeter also than honey and drippings of the honeycomb. Moreover, by them is your servant warned; in keeping them there is great reward (19:9–11).

5. The gospel is the greatest news ever sent. And pastors revel in believing it and telling it every day.

Even if our gospel is veiled, it is veiled to those who are perishing. In their case the god of this world has blinded the minds of the unbelievers, to keep them from seeing the light of the gospel of the glory of Christ, who is the image of God (2 Cor. 4:3–4).

To me, though I am the very least of all the saints, this grace was given, to preach to the Gentiles the unsearchable riches of Christ (Eph. 3:8).

I am under obligation both to Greeks and to barbarians, both to the wise and to the foolish. So I am eager to preach the gospel to you also who are in Rome (Rom. 1:14–15).

6. Corporate worship is the great overflow of life together in treasuring Christ. And pastors soar with the sacred privilege of feeling that weekly wonder and fanning that flame.

Let the word of Christ dwell in you richly, teaching and admonishing one another in all wisdom, singing psalms and hymns and spiritual songs, with thankfulness in your hearts to God (Col. 3:16).

I will thank you in the great congregation; in the mighty throng I will praise you (Ps. 35:18).

7. Faith is the great experience of union with Christ and the embrace of all God is for us in him. And pastors aim at this with every word, since faith comes by hearing and hearing by the Word of Christ.

I have been crucified with Christ. It is no longer I who live, but Christ who lives in me. And the life I now live in the flesh I live by faith in the Son of God, who loved me and gave himself for me (Gal. 2:20).

Convinced of this, I know that I will remain and continue with you all, for your progress and joy in the faith (Phil. 1:25).

8. Hope in future grace is the great furnace of gospel obedience. And pastors fuel it daily with the promises of God.

No unbelief made him waver concerning the promise of God, but he grew strong in his faith as he gave glory to God (Rom. 4:20).

You had compassion on those in prison, and you joyfully accepted the plundering of your property, since you knew that you yourselves had a better possession and an abiding one (Heb. 10:34).

Keep your life free from love of money, and be content with what you have, for he has said, "I will never leave you nor forsake you." So we can confidently say, "The Lord is my helper; I will not fear; what can man do to me?" (13:5–6).

9. Joy is the great impulse of gladness in pain and pleasure that makes its source in God look great. And pastors renounce all joy-destroying abuse and live for the holy joy of their flock.

   Rejoice in the Lord always; again I will say, rejoice (Phil. 4:4).

   Indeed, I count everything as loss because of the surpassing worth of knowing Christ Jesus my Lord (3:8).

   Not that we lord it over your faith, but we work with you for your joy (2 Cor. 1:24).

   As sorrowful, yet always rejoicing (6:10).

10. Love is the greatest act. And pastors make it the great aim of all their acts.

    Faith, hope, and love abide, these three; but the greatest of these is love (1 Cor. 13:13).

    The aim of our charge is love (1 Tim. 1:5).

    Owe no one anything, except to love each other, for the one who loves another has fulfilled the law (Rom. 13:8).

    Let all that you do be done in love (1 Cor. 16:14).

11. Holiness is great likeness to the thrice-holy God. And pastors daily kill their own sins for the sake of their own holiness and the holiness of others.

As he who called you is holy, you also be holy in all your conduct, since it is written, "You shall be holy, for I am holy" (1 Pet. 1:15–16).

For if you live according to the flesh you will die, but if by the Spirit you put to death the deeds of the body, you will live (Rom. 8:13).

Since we have these promises, beloved, let us cleanse ourselves from every defilement of body and spirit, bringing holiness to completion in the fear of God (2 Cor. 7:1).

12. Suffering is a great seminary. And pastors must attend it for the sake of their people.

Before I was afflicted I went astray, but now I keep your word. . . . It is good for me that I was afflicted, that I might learn your statutes (Ps. 119:67, 71).

If we are afflicted, it is for your comfort and salvation; and if we are comforted, it is for your comfort, which you experience when you patiently endure the same sufferings that we suffer (2 Cor. 1:6).

13. Explaining great truth is a path to great understanding—in the pastor! And pastors are charged to explain the greatest things relentlessly.

It is more blessed to give than to receive (Acts 20:35).

"You give them something to eat." They said to him, "We have only five loaves here and two fish." . . . And they took up twelve baskets full of the broken pieces left over (Matt. 14:16–17, 20).

And he gave the apostles, the prophets, the evangelists, the shepherds and teachers, to equip the saints for the work of ministry, for building up the body of Christ (Eph. 4:11–12).

14. Heralding the greatest realities is a great privilege. And pastors are the heralds of the living God.

I charge you in the presence of God and of Christ Jesus, who is to judge the living and the dead, and by his appearing and his kingdom: preach [herald!] the word (2 Tim. 4:1–2).

Therefore, we are ambassadors for Christ, God making his appeal through us. We implore you on behalf of Christ, be reconciled to God (2 Cor. 5:20).

15. Humanly impossible aims throw us on a great Helper. And all the spiritual aims of a pastor are impossible.

Those who heard it said, "Then who can be saved?" But he said, "What is impossible with man is possible with God" (Luke 18:26–27).

And the Lord's servant must not be quarrelsome but kind to everyone, able to teach, patiently enduring evil, correcting his opponents with gentleness. God may perhaps grant them repentance leading to a knowledge of the truth, and they may come to their senses and escape from the snare of the devil, after being captured by him to do his will (2 Tim. 2:24–26).

16. Heaven is a great destiny. And pastors aim in everything to help people get there.

Rejoice and be glad, for your reward is great in heaven (Matt. 5:12).

But our citizenship is in heaven, and from it we await a Savior, the Lord Jesus Christ, who will transform our lowly body to be like his glorious body, by the power that enables him even to subject all things to himself (Phil. 3:20–21).

I endure everything for the sake of the elect, that they also may obtain the salvation that is in Christ Jesus with eternal glory (2 Tim. 2:10).

17. Hell is a great danger. And pastors aim in everything to help people escape it.

Do not fear those who kill the body but cannot kill the soul. Rather fear him who can destroy both soul and body in hell (Matt. 10:28).

I have become all things to all people, that by all means I might save some (1 Cor. 9:22).

Wait for his Son from heaven, whom he raised from the dead, Jesus who delivers us from the wrath to come (1 Thess. 1:10).

18. Prayer is a path to the great presence and power of God. And pastors pray for their own souls and their flocks without ceasing.

Take . . . the sword of the Spirit, which is the word of God, praying at all times in the Spirit, with all prayer and supplication (Eph. 6:17–18).

Call upon me in the day of trouble; I will deliver you, and you shall glorify me (Ps. 50:15).

My heart's desire and prayer to God for them is that they may be saved (Rom. 10:1).

19. The new birth is a great miracle. And pastors are the ever-amazed midwives of God.

The wind blows where it wishes, and you hear its sound, but you do not know where it comes from or where it goes. So it is with everyone who is born of the Spirit (John 3:8).

I planted, Apollos watered, but God gave the growth. So neither he who plants nor he who waters is anything, but only God who gives the growth (1 Cor. 3:6–7).

You have been born again, not of perishable seed but of imperishable, through the living and abiding word of God. . . . And this word is the good news that was preached to you (1 Pet. 1:23–25).

20. Communion is the greatest supper. And pastors hold the sacred emblems in their very hands.

I have earnestly desired to eat this Passover with you before I suffer (Luke 22:15).

The cup of blessing that we bless, is it not a participation in the blood of Christ? The bread that we break, is it not a participation in the body of Christ? (1 Cor. 10:16).

21. Baptism is the greatest emblem of death and life. And pastors enact this drama on behalf of Christ.

Do you not know that all of us who have been baptized into Christ Jesus were baptized into his death? We were buried therefore with him by baptism into death, in order that, just as Christ was raised from the dead by the glory of the Father, we too might walk in newness of life (Rom. 6:3–4).

Go therefore and make disciples of all nations, baptizing them in the name of the Father and of the Son and of the Holy Spirit (Matt. 28:19).

22. Funerals offer a great vista of eternity. And pastors stand there full of hope with wide-eyed people.

So we are always of good courage. We know that while we are at home in the body we are away from the Lord, for we walk by faith, not by sight. Yes, we are of good courage, and we would rather be away from the body and at home with the Lord (2 Cor. 5:6–8).

Death is swallowed up in victory. O death, where is your victory? O death, where is your sting? The sting of death is sin, and the power of sin is the law. But thanks be to God, who gives us the victory through our Lord Jesus Christ (1 Cor. 15:54–57).

23. Weddings are God's great, life-long joining together of man and woman. And pastors put this drama on display for all to understand.

They are no longer two but one flesh. What therefore God has joined together, let not man separate (Matt. 19:6).

Wives, submit to your own husbands, as to the Lord. For the husband is the head of the wife even as Christ is the head of the church, his body, and is himself its Savior. Now as the church submits to Christ, so also wives should submit in everything to their husbands. Husbands, love your wives, as Christ loved the church and gave himself up for her (Eph. 5:22–25).

24. Hospital visits are a sacred imparting of great hope. And pastors mediate this holy transaction with their voice and hands.

Is anyone among you sick? Let him call for the elders of the church, and let them pray over him, anointing him with oil in the name of the Lord. And the prayer of faith will save the one who is sick, and the Lord will raise him up (James 5:14–15).

May the God of hope fill you with all joy and peace in believing, so that by the power of the Holy Spirit you may abound in hope (Rom. 15:13).

It happened that the father of Publius lay sick with fever and dysentery. And Paul visited him and prayed, and putting his hands on him healed him (Acts 28:8).

25. The devil is a great enemy. And pastors make holy war every day.

Be sober-minded; be watchful. Your adversary the devil prowls around like a roaring lion, seeking someone to devour. Resist him, firm in your faith (1 Pet. 5:8–9).

Submit yourselves therefore to God. Resist the devil, and he will flee from you (James 4:7).

26. Wise, biblical counsel is greater than much fine gold. And pastors make many rich.

A word fitly spoken is like apples of gold in a setting of silver (Prov. 25:11).

How much better to get wisdom than gold! To get understanding is to be chosen rather than silver (16:16).

Him we proclaim, warning everyone and teaching everyone with all wisdom, that we may present everyone mature in Christ (Col. 1:28).

27. World missions is the greatest enterprise in the world. And pastors preach and pray and agitate till all their people are goers or senders.

   And this gospel of the kingdom will be proclaimed throughout the whole world as a testimony to all nations, and then the end will come (Matt. 24:14).

   The harvest is plentiful, but the laborers are few; therefore pray earnestly to the Lord of the harvest to send out laborers into his harvest (9:37–38).

28. Loving money is the great root of countless evils. And pastors sever it in their souls and seek its cheerful death in all their flock.

   Those who desire to be rich fall into temptation, into a snare, into many senseless and harmful desires that plunge people into ruin and destruction. For the love of money is a root of all kinds of evils (1 Tim. 6:9–10).

   Godliness with contentment is great gain, for we brought nothing into the world, and we cannot take anything out of the world. But if we have food and clothing, with these we will be content (6:6–8).

   Each one must give as he has decided in his heart, not reluctantly or under compulsion, for God loves a cheerful giver (2 Cor. 9:7).

Keep your life free from love of money, and be content with what you have, for he has said, "I will never leave you nor forsake you" (Heb. 13:5).

29. Leadership in holy paths is the great need of all the sheep. And pastors wear this mantle humbly under the Great Shepherd.

Obey your leaders and submit to them, for they are keeping watch over your souls, as those who will have to give an account. Let them do this with joy and not with groaning, for that would be of no advantage to you (Heb. 13:17).

Now may the God of peace who brought again from the dead our Lord Jesus, the great shepherd of the sheep, by the blood of the eternal covenant, equip you with everything good that you may do his will, working in us that which is pleasing in his sight, through Jesus Christ, to whom be glory forever and ever. Amen (13:20–21).

30. Lowly servanthood is high greatness. And pastors rejoice to say: He must increase, and I must decrease.

Whoever would be great among you must be your servant (Mark 10:43).

He must increase, but I must decrease (John 3:30).

It is a great thing to be a pastor. This is my song of praise and thankfulness that, in great mercy, I was counted worthy to be entrusted with this office for so long. I pray that every seed I ever sowed would be even this day bearing fruit.

> The kingdom of God is as if a man should scatter seed on the ground. He sleeps and rises night and day, and the seed sprouts and grows; he knows not how. (Mark 4:26–27)

This is finally a tribute to the supremacy of God. He is great, not the preacher. But because he is, it is a great thing to be a pastor.

Yes, Lord, you must increase, because you are supreme in all things. In every part of pastoral ministry, you are supreme. I pray, therefore, that your name would be hallowed and your dominion established through every day's pastoral work, but especially through preaching. Lord, center the lives of all your shepherds on your holy Word and your all-glorious self. Fill them with truth and wonder and wisdom and power in the preaching of this great Word. May our pulpits be bright with the flame of your sovereign grace. And may we be faithful, in every lowly moment of application, night and day, to love our people and point them to the all-satisfying supremacy of yourself. I ask all of this, and more, because of the all-sufficient work of Jesus for the sake of needy pastors like us. Amen.

Conclusion

PEOPLE ARE STARVING FOR the grandeur of God. And the vast majority do not know it. Those who do, say, "O God, you are my God; earnestly I seek you; my soul thirsts for you; my flesh faints for you, as in a dry and weary land where there is no water" (Ps. 63:1). But most do not discern that they were made to thrill at the panorama of God's power and glory. They seek to fill the void in other ways. And even those who go to church—how many of them can say when they leave, "I have looked upon you in the sanctuary, beholding your power and glory" (v. 2)?

The glory of God is of infinite worth. It is the heart of what the apostles preached: "the light of the knowledge of the glory of God in the face of Jesus Christ" (2 Cor. 4:6). It is the goal of every Christian act: "whatever you do, do all to the glory of God" (1 Cor. 10:31). It is the focus of all Christian hope: "we rejoice in hope of the glory of God" (Rom. 5:2). It will someday replace the sun and moon as the light of life: "the city has no need of sun or moon to shine on it, for the glory of God gives it light" (Rev. 21:23). And even now, before that great day, "the heavens declare the glory of God" (Ps. 19:1). When people discover the worth of

God's glory—when God says, "Let there be light," and opens the eyes of the blind—they are like people who find a treasure hidden in a field and, full of joy, sell all they have to buy that field (Matt. 13:44). They are like Moses, who cried to the Lord, "Please show me your glory" (Exod. 33:18).

This is the heart-pang of every human being. Only a few know it. Only a few diagnose the longing beneath every human desire—the longing to see God. If only people could articulate the silent cry of their hearts! Would they not say, "One thing have I asked of the Lord, that I will seek after . . . to gaze upon the beauty of the Lord" (Ps. 27:4)? But instead, people "by their unrighteousness suppress the truth," and do "not see fit to acknowledge God," and even many who name the God of Israel have "changed their glory for that which does not profit" (Rom. 1:18, 28; Jer. 2:11).

Christian preachers, more than all others, should know this truth—that people are starving for God. If anyone in all the world should be able to say, "I have looked upon you in the sanctuary, beholding your power and glory," it is the herald of God. And as we look out over the wasteland of our secular culture, must we preachers not ask: Who but us will say to this people, "Behold your God!"? Who will tell the people that God is great and greatly to be praised? Who will paint for them the landscape of God's grandeur? Who will remind them with tales of wonder that God has triumphed over every foe? Who will cry out above every crisis, "Your God reigns!"? Who will labor to find words that can carry the "gospel of the glory of the blessed God"?

If God is not supreme in our preaching, where in this world will people hear about the supremacy of God? If we do not spread a banquet of God's beauty on Sunday morning, will not our people seek in vain to satisfy their inconsolable longing with the cotton candy pleasures of pastimes and religious hype? If the fountain of living water does not flow from the mountain of God's sovereign grace on Sunday morning, will not the people hew for themselves cisterns on Monday, "broken cisterns that can hold no water" (Jer. 2:13)?

We are called to be "stewards of the mysteries of God" (1 Cor. 4:1). And the great mystery is "Christ in you, the hope of glory" (Col. 1:27). And that glory is the glory of God. And "it is required of stewards that they be found faithful" (1 Cor. 4:2)—faithful in magnifying the supreme glory of the one eternal God. Not magnifying like a microscope that makes small things look bigger, but like a telescope that makes unimaginably great galaxies of glory visible to the human eye.

If we love our people, if we love the "other sheep" that are not yet gathered into the fold, if we love the fulfillment of God's global purpose, we will labor to "spread a table in the wilderness" (Ps. 78:19). People everywhere are starving for the enjoyment of God. For as Jonathan Edwards said:

> The enjoyment of God is the only happiness with which our souls can be satisfied. To go to heaven, fully to enjoy God, is infinitely better than the most pleasant accommodations here. Fathers and mothers, husbands, wives, or children, or the company of earthly friends, are but shadows; but God is the substance. These are but scattered beams, but God is the sun. These are but streams. But God is the ocean.[1]

A Word of Thanks

For the Revised and Expanded Edition

I WANT TO THANK BAKER BOOKS for their willingness to publish a third, expanded edition of *The Supremacy of God in Preaching*. I do not take for granted the fruitful partnership we have enjoyed in spreading this message for the last twenty-five years.

David Mathis, the executive editor of desiringGod.org, helped me choose and assemble material I had written since the last edition, so that I could rework it and expand it into the new chapters of this book. This new edition would not exist without his initiative and help.

Marshall Segal, my executive assistant, provides indispensable help behind the scenes every day, making it possible for me to do what I do. I would drown in a sea of administration and communication if he were not managing large parts of my life.

Finally, I thank God for the whole team at desiringGod.org. This is my first year actually on staff at Desiring God. Up till now I have worked for Bethlehem Baptist Church, and I still rejoice to dedicate this book to that flock. But in this new season of my life, my ministry is funded and sustained through the team

God has graciously assembled at Desiring God, and through the hundreds of partners who make that ministry possible.

For all these people and more, I am thankful. God has been very kind to me.

Notes

Preface to the Revised Edition

1. Jonathan Edwards, *The "Miscellanies,"* in *The Works of Jonathan Edwards*, vol. 13, ed. Thomas Schafer (New Haven: Yale University Press, 1994), 495, Miscellany #448. Emphasis added.

Preface to the First Edition

1. Andrew Bonar, ed., *Memoir and Remains of Robert Murray M'Cheyne* (Grand Rapids: Baker, 1978), 258.
2. Mark Noll, "Jonathan Edwards, Moral Philosophy, and the Secularization of American Christian Thought," *Reformed Journal* (February 1983): 26. Emphasis added.
3. Charles Colson, "Introduction," in Jonathan Edwards, *Religious Affections* (Sisters, OR: Multnomah, 1984), xxiii, xxxiv.
4. Iain Murray, *The Forgotten Spurgeon* (Edinburgh: Banner of Truth, 1966), 36.

Chapter 1: The Goal of Preaching

1. Charles H. Spurgeon, *Lectures to My Students* (Grand Rapids: Zondervan, 1972), 26.
2. James Stewart, *Heralds of God* (Grand Rapids: Baker, 1972), 73. This quote comes from William Temple, who formulated it to define worship, but Stewart borrowed it as giving "precisely the aims and ends of preaching."
3. John H. Jowett, *The Preacher: His Life and Work* (New York: Harper, 1912), 96, 98.
4. Spurgeon, *Lectures to My Students*, 146.
5. Samuel Johnson, *Lives of the English Poets* (London: Oxford University Press, 1906), 2:365.
6. Christopher Catherwood, *Five Evangelical Leaders* (Wheaton: Harold Shaw, 1985), 170.
7. Cotton Mather, *Student and Preacher, or Directions for a Candidate of the Ministry* (London: Hindmarsh, 1726), v.

8. An extended exegetical defense of this statement is given in John Piper, *Desiring God: Meditations of a Christian Hedonist*, 3rd ed. (Sisters, OR: Multnomah, 2003), appendix 1.
9. This is the thesis of *Desiring God*, where its implications for areas of life other than preaching are developed.

Chapter 2: The Ground of Preaching
1. For a defense and exposition of this definition, see John Piper, *The Justification of God: An Exegetical and Theological Study of Romans 9:1–23*, 2nd ed. (Grand Rapids: Baker, 1993).

Chapter 3: The Gift of Preaching
1. Phillips Brooks, *Lectures on Preaching* (Grand Rapids: Baker, 1969), 106.
2. Of course, the vast majority of the people of the world are not literate. The most urgent missionary preaching will not be the same form of preaching as is needed in most of the pulpits of America where Christians sit with Bibles in hand. Nevertheless, I want to make a case that even preaching to nonliterate peoples should include quoting much Scripture from memory and making clear that the authority of the preacher comes from an inspired book. Doing expository preaching for nonliterate cultures is a challenge that needs much attention.
3. Quoted in John R. W. Stott, *Between Two Worlds* (Grand Rapids: Eerdmans, 1982), 32.
4. Sereno Dwight, *Memoirs of Jonathan Edwards*, in *The Works of Jonathan Edwards*, vol. 1 (Edinburgh: Banner of Truth, 1974), xxi.
5. Quoted in Iain Murray, *The Forgotten Spurgeon* (Edinburgh: Banner of Truth, 1966), 34.

Chapter 4: The Gravity and Gladness of Preaching
1. Dwight, *Memoirs*, xx.
2. Jonathan Edwards, "The True Excellency of a Gospel Minister," in *The Works of Jonathan Edwards*, vol. 2 (Edinburgh: Banner of Truth, 1974), 958.
3. Jonathan Edwards, *The Great Awakening*, in *The Works of Jonathan Edwards*, vol. 4, ed. C. Goen (New Haven: Yale University Press, 1972), 272.
4. Dwight, *Memoirs*, clxxxix.
5. Ibid., cxc.
6. Stewart, *Heralds of God*, 102.
7. Andrew W. Blackwood, ed., *The Protestant Pulpit* (Grand Rapids: Baker, 1977), 311.
8. James W. Alexander, *Thoughts on Preaching* (Edinburgh: Banner of Truth, 1975), 264.
9. Brooks, *Lectures*, 82–83.
10. Bennet Tyler and Andrew Bonar, *The Life and Labors of Asahel Nettleton* (Edinburgh: Banner of Truth, 1975), 65, 67, 80.

11. Quoted in Stott, *Between Two Worlds*, 325.

12. Jowett, *The Preacher*, 89.

13. Bennet Tyler and Andrew Bonar, *The Life and Labors of Asahel Nettleton* (Edinburgh: Banner of Truth, 1975), 65, 67, 80.

14. William Sprague, *Lectures on Revivals of Religion* (Edinburgh: Banner of Truth, 1959), 119–20. The rest of this passage, though not included, is equally powerful.

15. Quoted in Murray, *Forgotten Spurgeon*, 38.

16. Spurgeon, *Lectures*, 212.

17. Quoted in Stewart, *Heralds of God*, 207.

18. Quoted in Charles Bridges, *The Christian Ministry* (Edinburgh: Banner of Truth, 1967), 214n2.

19. B. B. Warfield, "The Religious Life of Theological Students," in *The Princeton Theology*, ed. Mark Noll (Grand Rapids: Baker, 1983), 263.

20. Cited in Bridges, *The Christian Ministry*, 214.

21. Dwight, *Memoirs*, xx, xxii.

Chapter 5: Keep God Central

1. For readers interested in biographies of Edwards, I recommend: Iain Murray, *Jonathan Edwards: A New Biography* (Edinburgh: Banner of Truth, 1987), and George M. Marsden, *Jonathan Edwards: A Life* (New Haven: Yale University Press, 2003).

2. Dwight, *Memoirs*, xxxix.

3. Ibid., xxxviii.

4. Ibid., xx.

5. Ibid., xxxvi.

6. Ibid.

7. Elisabeth Dodds, *Marriage to a Difficult Man: The "Uncommon Union" of Jonathan and Sarah Edwards* (repr., Laurel, MS: Audubon Press, 2003), 20–21.

8. Jonathan Edwards, *Selections*, ed. C. H. Faust and T. Johnson (New York: Hill and Wang, 1962), 69

9. Dwight, *Memoirs*, clxxiv.

10. Ibid., clxxiv–clxxv.

11. Ibid., clxxvii.

12. Ibid., clxxix.

Chapter 6: Submit to Sweet Sovereignty

1. Jonathan Edwards, "The Sole Consideration, That God Is God, Sufficient to Still All Objections to His Sovereignty," in *The Works of Jonathan Edwards*, vol. 2 (Edinburgh: Banner of Truth, 1974), 107.

2. Ibid., 107–8.

3. Edwards, *Religious Affections*, 279.

4. Edwards, *Selections*, 69.

5. The complete text of *The End for Which God Created the World*, with explanatory notes, can be found in John Piper, *God's Passion for His Glory: Living the Vision of Jonathan Edwards* (Wheaton: Crossway, 1998).

6. Edwards, *Religious Affections*, 237.

7. Ibid., 243

8. Jonathan Edwards, *Miscellaneous Remarks Concerning Satisfaction for Sin*, in *The Works of Jonathan Edwards*, vol. 2, 569.

9. Jonathan Edwards, *Miscellaneous Remarks Concerning Faith*, in *The Works of Jonathan Edwards*, vol. 2, 588.

10. Ibid., 578–95. These observations and many similar reasonings are spread throughout Edwards's remarks in this section.

11. Jonathan Edwards, *Miscellaneous Remarks Concerning Efficacious Grace*, in *The Works of Jonathan Edwards*, vol. 2, 548.

12. Jonathan Edwards, *Miscellaneous Remarks Concerning Perseverance of the Saints*, in *The Works of Jonathan Edwards*, vol. 2, 596.

Chapter 7: Make God Supreme

1. Edwards, *Religious Affections*, 238.

2. Ibid., 244. Emphasis added.

3. Edwards, *Selections*, xx.

4. Jonathan Edwards, *Some Thoughts Concerning the Revival*, in *The Works of Jonathan Edwards*, vol. 4, ed. C. C. Goen (New Haven: Yale University Press, 1972), 387; see also 399.

5. Edwards, *Religious Affections*, 314

6. Ibid., 243.

7. Edwards, *Concerning the Revival*, 388.

8. Edwards, "True Excellency," 958.

9. Edwards, *Religious Affections*, 258.

10. Ibid., 289.

11. Edwards, *Concerning the Revival*, 386.

12. Edwards, "True Excellency," 959.

13. Edwards, "Personal Narrative," *Selections*, 65.

14. Dwight, *Memoirs*, xxi.

15. Ibid., clxxiv.

16. Edwards, "True Excellency," 957.

17. Dwight, *Memoirs*, ccxxx.

18. . Edwards, "Sinners in the Hands of an Angry God," in *The Works of Jonathan Edwards*, vol. 2, 10.

19. Quoted in John Gerstner, *Jonathan Edwards on Heaven and Hell* (Grand Rapids: Baker, 1980), 44. This volume gives an excellent introduction

to Edwards's balanced insights on the glories of heaven and the horrors of hell.

20. Edwards, *Religious Affections*, 259.

21. Edwards, *Perseverance*, in *The Works of Jonathan Edwards*, vol. 2, 596.

22. Edwards, *Religious Affections*, 308.

23. Edwards, *The Distinguishing Marks of a Work of the Spirit of God*, in *The Works of Jonathan Edwards*, vol. 4, 248.

24. Edwards, *Concerning the Revival*, 391.

25. Jonathan Edwards, *Freedom of the Will*, in *The Works of Jonathan Edwards*, vol. 2, 87.

26. Edwards, *Efficacious Grace*, 557.

27. Jonathan Edwards, *Pressing into the Kingdom*, in *The Works of Jonathan Edwards*, vol. 1, 659.

28. Dwight, *Memoirs*, clxxxix.

29. Ibid., xxx.

30. Ibid.

31. Ibid., clxxxix.

32. Edwards, *Religious Affections*, 246.

33. Edwards, "True Excellency," 957.

34. Edwards, *Concerning the Revival*, 390–91.

35. Edwards, "The Most High, A Prayer-Hearing God," in *The Works of Jonathan Edwards*, vol. 2, 116.

36. Edwards, *Concerning the Revival*, 438.

37. Edwards, "True Excellency," 960.

38. Edwards, "Personal Narrative," *Selections*, 61.

39. Edwards, *A Humble Attempt*, in *The Works of Jonathan Edwards*, vol. 2, 278–312.

40. Edwards, *Religious Affections*, 302.

41. Ibid., 308.

42. Edwards, "Christ the Example of Ministers," in *The Works of Jonathan Edwards*, vol. 2, 961.

43. Edwards, "Personal Narrative," *Selections*, 69.

44. Ibid., 67.

45. Quoted in *The Great Awakening*, in *The Works of Jonathan Edwards*, vol. 4, 72.

46. See the illustration quoted above, pp. 54–55.

47. Dwight, *Memoirs*, cxc.

48. Horatius Bonar, "Preface," in John Gillies, *Historical Collections of Accounts of Revival* (Edinburgh: Banner of Truth, 1981), vi.

49. Edwards, *Concerning the Revival*, 386.

Chapter 8: Jonathan Edwards Thirty-Three Years Later

1. Edwards, *The "Miscellanies,"* 495, Miscellany #448; see also #87, pp. 251–52; #332, p. 410; #679 (not in the New Haven volume). Emphasis added.

2. Jonathan Edwards, "521. Luke 22:44," Sermons, Series II, 1739 (WJE Online vol. 54), ed. Jonathan Edwards Center, accessed February 18, 2014, http://edwards.yale.edu/archive?path=aHR0cDovL2Vkd2FyZ HMueWFsZS5lZHUvY2dpLWJpbi9uZXdwaGGlsby9nZXRvYmplY3Q ucGw/ Yy41MjoyMS53amVv.

3. Jonathan Edwards, "Approaching the End of God's Grand Design," in *The Works of Jonathan Edwards*, vol. 25, ed. Wilson Kimnach (New Haven: Yale University Press, 2006), 111–26.

4. Ibid, 116.

5. Ibid.

6. Ibid.

7. Ibid., 116–17.

8. My most extended gathering of texts on this point is John Piper, *Let the Nations Be Glad: The Supremacy of God in Missions* (Grand Rapids: Baker Academic, 2010), 40–46.

9. Edwards, "Approaching the End of God's Grand Design," 117.

10. Ibid., 118.

11. Edwards is careful to express union with Christ in a way that does not imply our becoming God. "[Union with Christ] is expressed in Scripture by the saints being made 'partakers of divine nature' (2 Peter 1:4), and having God dwelling in them, and they in God. . . . Not that the saints are made partakers of the essence of God, and so are 'Godded' with God, and 'Christed' with Christ, according to the abominable and blasphemous language and notions of some heretics; but, to use the Scripture phrase, they are made partakers of God's fullness (*Ephesians 3:17–19, John 1:16*), that is, of God's spiritual beauty and happiness, according to the measure and capacity of a creature." Jonathan Edwards, *The Religious Affections*, in *The Works of Jonathan Edwards*, vol. 2, 203.

12. Robert Letham, *Union with Christ: In Scripture, History, and Theology* (Phillipsburg, NJ: P&R Publishing, 2011): "Union with Christ is crucial to, and at the heart of, the biblical teaching about salvation," (p. 3), "Nothing is more central or basic than union with and communion with Christ," (p. 1).

13. Edwards, "Approaching the End of God's Grand Design," 116–17, emphasis added.

Chapter 9: In Honor of Tethered Preaching

1. John Calvin, *Commentary on the Gospel According to John*, vol. 2, trans. William Pringle (repr., Grand Rapids: Baker, 2003), 182.

2. John Calvin, "Letter to Cardinal Jacopo Sadoleto," quoted in J. H. Merle D'Aubigne, *Let Christ Be Magnified* (Edinburgh: Banner of Truth, 2007), 13.

3. To give you some idea of the scope of Calvin's pulpit, he began his series on the book of Acts on August 25, 1549, and ended it in March 1554. After Acts

he went on to the epistles to the Thessalonians (46 sermons), Corinthians (186 sermons), pastorals (86 sermons), Galatians (43 sermons), Ephesians (48 sermons)—till May 1558. Then there was a gap when he was ill. In the spring of 1559 he began his Harmony of the Gospels and was not finished when he died in May 1564. For these and more statistics see T. H. L. Parker, *Portrait of Calvin* (Philadelphia: Westminster Press, 1954), 83; and W. de Greef, *The Writings of John Calvin: An Introductory Guide*, trans. Lyle D. Bierma (Grand Rapids: Baker, 1993), 111–12.

Conclusion

1. Jonathan Edwards, "The Christian Pilgrim," in *The Works of Jonathan Edwards*, vol. 2, 244.

General Index

contemporary preaching, 29
contextualization, 129, 133
contrition, 84
corporate worship, 138
creation, 118
crises of our day, 28
criticism, 21
cultural relativism, 48
culture, 20, 123

Dale, Robert, 28
death, 42, 63, 69
decrees, of God, 131
delight, 83–84, 137
Denney, James, 63
diet, 75
discouragement, 21
Dissertation Concerning the End for Which God Created the World (Edwards), 83, 114, 166
doctrine, 116
Donne, John, 66
doxology, 72
Dwight, Sereno, 57, 94, 100, 101

earnestness, 55–59, 66, 106
Edwards, Jonathan
on death, 69
on glory of God, 13–14
"God-entranced worldview" of, 20
joy of, 62, 153
life and ministry of, 73–79
as model pastor, 11, 71–72
preaching of, 55–59, 87–109
on Scripture, 50, 124
theology of, 81–86
thirty-three years later, 113–22
on union with Christ, 162
Edwards, Sarah, 73–74

efficiency, 75
elitism, 28
eloquence, 108
emotions, 14, 56, 77, 83, 88, 91
emptiness, 106
entertainment, 123, 126, 128
eternal security, 67
eternity, 145
euangelizomenōn agatha, 30
evangelicals, 20, 48
exercise, 75
experimental religion, 102
expository preaching, 15, 158
extra-biblical illustrations, 127
exultation, 14, 84, 106

faith, 84–85, 139
false security, 107
fear, 96–97
feeling, 15
Finney, Charles, 64
Flavel, John, 69
flesh, 133
Freedom of the Will, The (Edwards), 99, 114
fruit, 89
funerals, 69, 145–46
future grace, 139

Gerstner, John, 160
Gillies, John, 108
gladness, 60, 67
God
all-sufficiency of, 82
decrees of, 131
dominion of, 29–31
glory of, 13–14, 18, 32–33, 37, 39, 47, 68, 83, 117, 119, 132, 151–53

greatness of, 18–19, 136
holiness of, 17–18, 27, 29, 81, 82
mercy of, 103
power of, 47
providence of, 26
righteousness of, 36, 37, 38
seeing and savoring of, 14–15
self-communication of, 118–19
supremacy of, 11, 106, 150, 152
good news, 30, 35, 127, 138
Gordon-Conwell Theological Seminary, 20, 26
gospel, 33, 40, 61, 130, 138
gratitude, 84
gravity, of preaching, 55–60, 62, 66, 67
Great Awakening, 76–77, 87, 101, 104
grief, 84
guilt, 96–97, 106
Gurnall, William, 69

happiness, 60
Harold John Ockenga Lectures on Preaching, 26
heart, 100–103
heaven, 63, 67, 95, 97, 107, 143, 161
"Heaven Is a World of Love" (Edwards), 96
hell, 56, 63, 67, 70, 95, 96, 97, 100, 107, 143, 161
helplessness, 106
heralding, 14, 30, 142
history, 118
holiness, of God, 17–18, 19, 27, 29, 67, 81, 82, 96, 140–41
holy affections, 88–90

Holy Spirit
and contextualization, 129–30, 133
dependence on, 45
gift of, 47–50
as Helper, 137, 142
inspiration of, 49
power of, 50–53
and prayer, 103–4
hope, 139
hospital visitation, 146–47
humility, 37, 40–43, 49, 52, 106, 127
humor, 63, 65–66, 70
hyper-Calvinism, 98

illustrations, 127
image of God, 36
images, 94–96
indifference, 132
inerrancy, 48
Institutes of the Christian Religion (Calvin), 94
intensity, 107–9
interpretation, 49
introspection, 101
irresistible grace, 98

Jesus Christ
centrality of, 117–18
cross of, 37–43
example of, 70
as gentle and lowly, 104
greatness of, 136
lordship of, 32–33
suffering of, 120
Johnson, Samuel, 28–29
John the Baptist, 70, 90
jokes, 55, 62
Jowett, John Henry, 28, 63

Scripture Index